Faith
ESSENTIALS

Todd Gaddis

WORLD WIDE
PUBLISHING GROUP

7710-T Cherry Park Drive, Ste 224
Houston, TX 77095
713-766-4271
www.WorldwidePublishingGroup.com

Paperback: 978-1-68411-168-8
Hardcover: 978-1-68411-183-1

Table of Contents

1: Dynamite 1

2: In the Beginning.. 9

3: Someone with a Face.. 17

4: Paradise Postponed... 25

5: 3:16 to Eternity... 33

6: "The Music is in Me" 41

7: Constant Contact 49

8: Upon this Rock 59

9: Throw Out the Lifeline... 69

10: "Look! Water!".. 77

11: Misconceptions about Giving 85

12: God's Messengers... 93

13: "It Sure is Hot Down Here!" 103

14: Something Better... 111

15: "I Shall Return" 119

16: Worthless Stubble or Costly Stones? 127

17: The Second Death.. 135

18: Paradise Restored 143

19: The Great Commandment 153

ENDNOTES 161

1

DYNAMITE

"All Scripture is inspired by God …"
(2 Timothy 3:16).

෮෮෬

Mahatma Gandhi, a committed Hindu and preeminent leader of India's independence movement from British rule in the mid- 20th century, spoke forcefully to Christians when he said: "You Christians have in your keeping a document with enough dynamite in it to blow the whole of civilization to bits; to turn society upside down; to bring peace to this war-torn world. But you read it as if it were just good literature, and nothing else."[1]

Good literature certainly describes the Bible, which covers such subjects as religion, history, poetry, and science. Written by 40 authors over a span of 1500 years, it is far and away the best-selling book of all time. Yet, even as an unbeliever like Gandhi readily admitted, the power it contains far outweighs any temporal, earthly review and description one could give it.

The Holy Bible stands in a class by itself because it's **God's Word.** The apostle Paul reminds us that, *"All Scripture is inspired by God …"* (2 Timothy 3:16). Nothing else penned throughout history can be

1

described in such a way. Numerous books centered on other faiths besides Christianity have been written and taught over the centuries, yet they have people as their source and not God.

W.C. Fields, the famous comic and lifetime agnostic was discovered by someone reading through a Bible on his deathbed. "Why are you reading the Bible?" they questioned. "I am looking for loopholes," he answered. God's perfect Word contains no loopholes. It says what it means and means what it says. With this vital truth in place, join me in a journey that symbolizes the multiple ways in which Scripture can be described.

First, the Bible is an **instruction manual.** While that may sound a bit dry, don't underestimate its importance.

Most people know me as not being mechanically inclined, yet I *can* follow directions when necessary. When we began having trouble with our television remote recently, I called the company and soon received a replacement. I opened the box, carefully adhered to the enclosed instructions and quickly got it working. Had the directions not been carefully spelled out, I would not have been successful.

"ALL SCRIPTURE IS PROFITABLE"

Likewise, how can we expect to live the Christian life without following detailed, written guidelines? Fortunately, God has provided us with these through His Word. As Paul goes on to say: *"All Scripture is inspired by God and profitable for teaching, for reproof, for correction, for training in righteousness"* (2 Timothy 3:16).

Like providing directions for believers in Jesus Christ, God's Word serves as a **rule book**. The Ten Commandments come to mind as the most obvious example, but let us not forget the Golden Rule from the lips of our Lord Himself that commands us to *do unto others as we would have them do unto us* (Matthew 7:12).

I have enjoyed watching and playing golf for most of my life. Golf is a game that calls for following strict guidelines and proper etiquette. In fact, you can go online and find the most recent United States Golf Association rules, nearly 200 pages of them! Most amateurs probably don't know all the rules, but you can bet the professionals earning a living at the game do.

As a society we've become increasingly adept at bending, even breaking the rules. Tragically, such behavior infiltrates the church. Being a Christian means so much more than following a bunch of regulations, yet, that doesn't give us license to violate the guidelines God has given.

Along this same vein, Scripture can be compared to a **road map.** The Bible says, *"Establish my footsteps in Your word, And do not let any iniquity have dominion over me"* (Psalms 119:133). We can't expect to have our footsteps grounded in His Word if we aren't reading and listening to it. Just like those maps under my couch are tattered and worn, my Bible should show evidence of my having spent time there – okay, phones and tablets count, too! Ronnie Reno and Don Schroeder understood this connection decades ago when they wrote the Gospel/country song, "I'm Using my Bible for a Roadmap."

Note also that God's Word is a **guiding light.** Scripture says, *"Your word is a lamp to my feet and a light to my path"* (Psalm 119:105). This brings to mind a recent, harrowing experience. I was driving down a narrow, winding, rural road on a rainy evening after dark. Imagine my panic when I accidently turned off the headlights instead of turning on the wipers. As important as this illumination was on that black night, our need for God's direction through His Word in this dark, fallen world is infinitely greater. Perhaps this account by Frank Koch in the *U.S. Naval Institute Proceedings* makes that point clearer:

> Two battleships assigned to the training squadron had been at sea on maneuvers in heavy weather for several days. I was serving on the lead battleship and was on

watch on the bridge as night fell. The visibility was poor with patchy fog, so the captain remained on the bridge keeping an eye on all activities.

Shortly after dark, the lookout on the wing reported, "Light, bearing on the starboard bow." "Is it steady or moving astern?" the captain called out. The lookout replied, "Steady, Captain," which meant we were on a dangerous collision course with that ship.

The captain then called to the signalman, "Signal that ship: 'We are on a collision course, advise you to change course twenty degrees.'" Back came the signal, "Advisable for you to change course twenty degrees."

The captain said, "Send: 'I'm a captain, change course twenty degrees.'" "I'm a seaman second-class," came the reply. "You had better change course twenty degrees."

By that time the captain was furious. He spat out, "Send: 'I'm a battleship. Change course twenty degrees.'" Back came the flashing light, "I'm a lighthouse." We changed course.[2]

Scripture serves as a spiritual beacon, a guiding light, keeping us on the right course while guarding against our drifting off on the wrong one.

It functions also as a **blazing fire.** What does a fire do? It *heats,* providing warmth and comfort. It *melts,* turning solids into liquids. It *purifies,* burning away impurities. It *energizes,* moving the motionless. It *ignites,* kindling the lifeless.

This description reminds me of this vivid testimony from one of the Major Prophets: *"His word is in my heart like a fire, a fire shut up in my bones"* (Jeremiah 20:9, NIV). The call of God upon his life and Word of God in his heart so convinced and compelled Jeremiah that he couldn't help but pass it along to the people.

"SHARPER THAN A TWO-EDGED SWORD"

Many times, I've sat down for sermon preparation distracted and unmotivated, yet knowing I've got to put together something by Sunday. Thankfully, duty becomes delight as God's Word radiates through my mind, soul, and spirit. Later, I step confidently behind the pulpit and gaze upon the congregation with eager anticipation, not because of talent and preparation on my part but because of truth and inspiration that come from the Lord.

Next, see that Scripture works like a **surgical instrument**. As the Bible says, *"For the word of God is living and active and sharper than any two-edged sword, and piercing as far as the divisions of soul and spirit, of both joints and marrow, and able to judge the thoughts and intentions of the heart"* (Hebrews 4:12).

In March of 2015, I underwent a lateral epicondylectomy, otherwise known as tennis elbow surgery. Out of curiosity, I later watched another patient on YouTube going through the same procedure, cringing as the doctor made a two-inch incision and cut his way down to the problem area.

As sharp as that 15-blade scalpel was, Scripture is infinitely sharper. The Holy Spirit, with God's Word in hand, pierces and penetrates our façade, boring deeply into our hearts with divine truth. This procedure is so precise and intricate that God can peel away the outer layer of pretension and expose our inner thoughts, motives, and intentions. Whereas my orthopedic surgeon got a good look at muscle, tissue, ligament, and bone in my body, the Great Physician uses His Word to mine deeply into my soul and spirit.

Note, too, that the Bible is **food for the soul.** Menelik II, one of the greatest rulers in African history, served as king of Shewa and emperor of Ethiopia during a time of great expansion (1889-1913). He thwarted an Italian invasion at the great Battle of Adwa and spearheaded a significant program of modernization. Despite his success, he had one, little-known eccentricity that led to his demise.

Thinking the Bible had curative powers, he ate a few pages whenever he felt ill. He died in 1913 after consuming the entire book of Kings.

Perhaps these words influenced him. *"How sweet are Your words to my taste! Yes sweeter than honey to my mouth!* (Psalm 119:103), or maybe this verse: *"Your words were found and I ate them"* (Jeremiah 15:16).

Rather than eat them literally, like Menelik II, we should ingest and digest them figuratively, allowing them to feed the soul and nourish our spirit. As Jesus said, *"MAN SHALL NOT LIVE ON BREAD ALONE, BUT ON EVERY WORD THAT PROCEEDS OUT OF THE MOUTH OF GOD"* (Matthew 4:4). This is why fasting is such an important spiritual discipline. As our physical hunger intensifies, we become increasingly sensitive to the Word of God and voice of the Spirit, especially when combining our efforts with prayer.

"GOD'S LOVE LETTER"

God's Word can also be described as a **love letter.** In some translations of Scripture, the word "love" appears over 500 times. This comes as no surprise, knowing that God's love for us and our need to love one another is one of the Bible's major messages.

One of my most treasured possessions is a bundle of love letters that my wife and I exchanged while dating and engaged in 1982-83. Since email and cell phones didn't exist, we either wrote or talked long distance, which got expensive at several cents a minute.

As special as these 35-year-old mementos are, they pale in comparison to God's centuries old love letter, otherwise known as the Holy Bible. I often tell my congregation, "There's nothing you can do to make God love you any more, there's nothing you can do to make God love you any less."

Why do I make such a claim? Because God's Word tells me His love is unconditional. *"For God so loved the world that He gave His only begotten Son"* (John 3:16). He *"demonstrates His own love toward us, in that while we were yet sinners, Christ died for us"* (Romans 5:8, emphasis added).

Understand the Bible too as a **crystal ball.** This suggests visualizing the future, which is exactly what the Word does.

God told Abram what would happen to his descendants four hundred years down the road (Genesis 15:13). Micah prophesied that Bethlehem would be the site of Jesus birth (Micah 5:2). Centuries before it happened, Isaiah detailed how Jesus would ultimately suffer for our sins (Isaiah 53).

While these and many other events spelled out in the Word have already occurred, numerous others are recorded that have yet to take place. I don't get too worked up over bad things that happen in the world because God's "crystal ball" tells me our side wins in the end. When I die, I'm going to what the Bible describes as a beautiful and restful place called heaven. Jesus is coming a second time and bringing the saints who have died with Him. In the end, this planet as we know it will be destroyed by fire, after which Christ will reign over a new heaven and new earth (more on these subjects in later chapters).

Finally, observe that Scripture can be characterized as a **life saver.** *"For by grace you have been saved through faith"* (Ephesians 2:8). This faith *"comes from hearing, and hearing by the word of Christ"* (Romans 10:17). Maybe you weren't reading the Bible directly when you came to know Jesus as your Savior. Nevertheless, no one is saved apart from God's Word.

> A missionary was standing on the street of a city in Africa with a small New Testament in his hand. An African man approached him and asked if he could have the little book. The missionary was not reluctant to part with the testament, but he was curious to why the man wanted it.
>
> "Its pages are the perfect size for rolling cigarettes," the man confessed.

The missionary was impressed with the honesty of the African and decided to extend a challenge. "I will give you this book if you will read every word on every page before you roll a cigarette with it," said the missionary. The African accepted the challenge and was given the New Testament.

About fifteen years later the missionary went to a revival being preached by an African evangelist. When the black evangelist saw the white man, he approached him and said, "You don't remember me, do you?"

"No," said the missionary. "Have we met before?"

"Yes, fifteen years ago you gave me a New Testament and made me promise to read every word on the page before I rolled a cigarette with it. It took me from Matthew's Gospel until the third chapter of John before I quit smoking the Word and started preaching it. That New Testament is the reason I'm here to preach the Word tonight!"

You don't have to smoke the Bible in order for it to make a change in your life like that of this African man. Yet you do have to believe and embrace it. Allow it to come in through your eyes and ears and find its way into your heart. Why? Because your birth and growth in the Kingdom depend on it. It serves as a foundation, springboard, and launching pad for all chapters which follow. Experience its dynamite power that exceeds anything this world offers.

2

IN THE BEGINNING

"In the beginning God . . ."
(Genesis 1:1).

ಬಿಂ

A kindergarten teacher gave her class a blank piece of paper and told them to draw something important to them. Several minutes later, every student except one had turned in their work. Little Johnny was still coloring at his desk in the back of the room. The teacher curiously walked to him, put her hand on his shoulder and asked, "Johnny, what are you drawing?"

"God," he said, without looking up.

"But Johnny," she kindly replied, "No one knows what God looks like."

"They will when I'm through," he replied.

Although you won't know what God looks like when you finish this chapter, hopefully you'll have learned more about Him.

First, **what does God do?**

God *creates*, both *originally* and on an *ongoing* basis. The very first chapter in the Bible, Genesis 1, provides a detailed account of creation's formation. (This would be a good time to listen to or read these 31 verses.)

And even though *"the heavens and the earth were completed, and all their hosts"* (Genesis 2:1) at this point, common sense and careful observation tell us that He didn't stop creating. Astronomers have learned new stars are continually being created throughout the universe. Naturalists claim new species are emerging. Above all else, people, God's crown jewel, are conceived by the hundreds of thousands across the globe daily.

God not only creates, He **sustains.** In 2000, I moved into a newly constructed home, the first and only one my wife and I have ever owned. After 16 years (we still live there, by the way), I have discovered that building the house was only the beginning of ownership responsibility. Maintaining the property, things such as taxes, utilities, routine maintenance, yard work, etc. are just as important as the initial purchase.

Creating this earth was only the beginning for God. Thousands of years have passed and He continues to sustain everything He has made. And since He loves people more than any other part of His creation, God devotes special attention to those who are part of His kingdom here on earth. As Scripture challenges, *"Cast your burden upon the LORD, and He will sustain you; He will never allow the righteous to be shaken"* (Psalm 55:22).

"GOD IS A PERSON"

Secondly, **who is God?**

He is a **person,** possessing intellect, feelings, and will. I know this because His Word says, *"God created man in His own image, in the image of God He created him"* (Genesis 1:27). The night before His crucifixion, Jesus said *"He who has seen Me has seen the Father"* (John 14:9).

Clearly, God is a person. In fact, He is **three people,** the Father, Son, and Holy Spirit. However, we must use caution when using the three-person explanation because it could imply separate moral or rational individuals. "There are not *three individuals but three personal self-distinctions* within *one* divine essence."[1] Terms used to describe this divine trio are *Trinity* and *triune.* As that great hymn of the faith, *Holy, Holy, Holy* proclaims, "God in three persons, blessed Trinity."

The term "Trinity" never appears in Scripture, though it is clearly implied. Jesus commissioned His disciples to baptize new converts *"in the name of the Father and the Son, and the Holy Spirit"* (Matthew 28:19). Paul writes, *"The grace of the Lord Jesus Christ, and the love of God, and the fellowship of the Holy Spirit, be with you all"* (2 Corinthians 13:14).

"It is important to understand the relationships of the persons of the Trinity. The Son and the Spirit are said to be 'subordinate' to the Father, but this does not mean they are inferior. Their subordination has been called a matter or relationship but not of nature."[2]

If you have trouble wrapping your mind around this, think of an egg. Though it's made up of a shell, yolk, and egg white, it's still one egg. Think of the Father, the fount of Deity, as the one who *originates;* the Son, eternally begotten of the Father, as the one who *reveals;* and the Spirit, eternally proceeding from the Father and the Son, as the one who *executes.*[3] They each have separate roles to play, but will never act independently of one another.

And finally, **what is God?**

God is Spirit, which implies that He is invisible, not possessing a physical body. As Jesus said to a curious follower, *"God is spirit, and* *those who worship Him must worship in spirit and truth"* (John 4:24). Paul writes that Jesus *"is the image of the invisible God,"* (Colossians 1:15), and *"Now to the King eternal, immortal, invisible, the only God,"* (1 Timothy 1:17).

Many find this difficult because they desire to worship something or someone they can see. And that's where faith comes in. Like the Bible says, *"Faith is the assurance of things hoped for, the conviction of things not seen"* (Hebrews 11:1).

God is Holy. Holy means sacred and set apart, which certainly describes God. "Holiness is the sum total of the perfection of God, perhaps the most comprehensive of all of God's attributes."[4] Moses and the Israelites sang immediately upon escaping the Egyptians and crossing the Red Sea, *"Who is like you among the gods, O LORD? Who is like You, majestic in holiness?"* (Exodus 15:11).

Everything God does is good, perfect, and right. He is not tempted by evil. In fact, as one of the minor prophets writes, *"Your eyes are too pure to approve evil"* (Habakkuk 1:13).

Why did Christ cry out from the cross, *"MY GOD, MY GOD, WHY HAVE YOU FORSAKEN ME?"* (Matthew 27:46), when He had never sinned? He cried out because He took on our sin. And as a result, for those brief moments in time, that perfect union between Father and Son was interrupted because a Holy God could not even look at sin.

God is omnipotent, all powerful, which means there is nothing He can't do. *"Ah Lord GOD! Behold, You have made the heavens and the earth by Your great power and Your outstretched arm! Nothing is too difficult for You"* acknowledged Jeremiah, even while imprisoned! (Jeremiah 32:17). As the angel Gabriel assured when the Virgin Mary questioned the possibility of her giving birth to a Son, *"For nothing will be impossible with God"* (Luke 1:37).

A young boy was studying his Sunday school lesson while flying to visit his grandparents. An observant, sympathetic passenger sitting next to him said, "Young man, if you can tell me something God can do, I'll give you a big, shiny apple." The boy thought a moment and then replied, "Mister, if you can tell me something God can't do, I'll give you a whole barrel of apples!"

Have you found yourself in an impossible situation, facing insurmountable odds? The next time this happens, begin celebrating and anticipating because you are in the best position to experience God's good work. There's nothing He can't do.

See too, that **God is omnipresent, in all places at all times.** As I write these words, I have one daughter and son-in law four hours away in a neighboring state and another daughter and son-in law 7,000 miles away in South Korea. I don't see them as much as I'd like because I'm not near them. Yet, I take comfort knowing that God is near them.

"YOU ARE THERE"

David asked and answered, *"Where can I go from Your Spirit? Or where can I flee from Your presence? If I ascend to heaven, You are there; If I make my bed in Sheol, behold, You are there. If I take the wings of the dawn, If I dwell in the remotest part of the sea, even there Your hand will lead me, And Your right hand will lay hold of me"* (Psalm 139:7-10).

Jesus told His disciples the night before the crucifixion that it was to their advantage that He leave them. What could be better than having Jesus physically with them? The answer is having the Holy Spirit spiritually there with them. Jesus, constrained by time and space, could not be everywhere at once. The third member of the Trinity, the Spirit, would be always in them and around them, comforting, convicting, and guiding.

Note, as well, that God is **omniscient, all knowing.** He not only hears our words; He knows our thoughts even before we think them. He has the very hairs of our heads numbered, which for me is getting fewer by the day.

David said to God, *"You know when I sit down and when I rise up"* (Psalm 139:2). We read this about Christ when He was challenged by the Pharisees for healing a demon-possessed man: *"And knowing their thoughts Jesus said to them, 'Any kingdom divided against itself is laid waste; and any city or house divided against itself will not stand"* (Matthew 12:25). This is just one of the many times, as fully God, that Jesus demonstrated His omniscient capabilities.

Observe also, that **God is immutable, unchanging.** In my 26 years as a pastor, I've been heartbroken on those rare but saddening occasions when someone to whom I was very close turned against me. No doubt, some of those who shouted *"Hosanna in the highest"* (Mark 11:9) when Jesus made His entry into Jerusalem, screamed *"Crucify Him!"* (Mark 15:14) days later. One can only imagine the pain Jesus must have felt when one of His dearest friends, Peter, denied even knowing Him.

Thankfully, God doesn't vacillate. That's hard to wrap our minds around in a world where things constantly change. Yet the Bible confirms this truth. As God spoke through one of His prophets, *"For I, the LORD, do not change"* (Malachi 3:6). *"Jesus Christ is the same, yesterday and today and forever"* (Hebrews 13:8). According to our Lord's half-brother, *"Every good thing given and every perfect gift is from above, coming down from the Father of lights, with who there is no variation or shifting shadow"* (James 1:17).

Not only is God unwavering, but **He is eternal.** Simply said, there has never been a time when He did not exist. Since He created time, He was obviously there before it existed. He was, is, and always will be.

Every human being has a beginning, but no end. Each of us will spend eternity somewhere. One hundred million years from now, our souls will still be alive, either in heaven or hell. The choice is ours, as we'll later see.

God, on the other hand, is an eternal being with neither a beginning nor end. As Scripture says, *"The eternal God is a dwelling place"* (Deuteronomy 33:27).

Next, understand that **God is sovereign.** *"But our God is in the heavens; He does whatever He pleases"* (Psalm 115:3). He controls everything in the universe, governing all that happens. Nothing can place a limitation on Him. He does, however, place limitations on Himself.

He will never nullify the free will of people. He created Adam and Eve and placed them in Eden. He gave them instructions but didn't program them to obey. Adam and Eve made a choice to sin. It was their decision to eat the forbidden fruit, thus bringing about the Fall.

He will not act contrary to His own nature. God can never call evil good, withhold His love, or leave sin unpunished.

"To the finite mind it is impossible to harmonize the sovereignty of God and the free will of man. But in the infinite mind of God there is no conflict. Finite minds can only accept both as facts and experience. The sovereignty of God never violates man's freedom. But it does require responsibility in man's choices."[5]

A clear example of God's sovereignty is found in the life of Jacob's favorite son Joseph. Although his brothers sold him into slavery, Joseph ended up second-in-command to the Pharaoh in Egypt, wisely navigating the region through years of horrific famine. Joseph could have enacted revenge when reuniting with his brothers. Instead, he forgave them, saying, *"You meant evil against me, but God meant it for good to bring about this present result, to preserve many people alive"* (Genesis 50:20). Joseph's abduction eventually brought about the fulfillment of prophecy, as Jacob relocated his entire family to the land of Goshen in Egypt, where they grew in number from 70 to over two million. After 400 years of slavery and oppression (Genesis 15:13), Moses led them to the Promised Land.

"MY THOUGHTS ARE NOT YOUR THOUGHTS"

Perhaps you find yourself enslaved in a difficult circumstance. On the surface, nothing makes sense. You've prayed for relief, yet nothing changes. Consider the possibility, like with Joseph, God has something much bigger in mind. It doesn't make sense now, but it will.

"'For My thoughts are not your thoughts, Nor are your ways My ways,' *declares the Lord."* (Isaiah 55:8). As Paul writes, *"God causes all things to work together for good to those who love God, to those called according to His purpose"* (Romans 8:28). His eternal sovereignty trumps our temporal situations every time.

Finally, *"**God is love**"* (1 John 4:8). Note that this verse doesn't say "God loves," separating the action from Himself. One might question, "doesn't God love?" Absolutely! Yet His love is so pure, intense, and unconditional, it cannot be distinguished from who He is.

> A simple peasant believer once had a weather vane on top of his barn on which were inscribed the words, "God is love." One day an infidel came to visit him and on seeing this weathervane changing position in the wind he turned to the peasant and with a ridiculing smile upon his face said, "You mean to say that your God is as changeable as the wind?" The peasant shook his head. "No," he said, "What I mean to say is that no matter which way the wind blows, God is love!" The infidel was put to shame.[6]

Considering how powerful God is and the many wonderful things He has done, nothing compares to His crowning achievement described in the next chapter.

3

SOMEONE WITH A FACE

"He who has seen Me has seen the Father"
(John 14:9).

୫୦୯ଓ

A little boy, scared of the shadows in his room, called for his mother. "God is there with you," she gently answered. "Yes, I know," responded the boy, "but I want someone with a face!"

Over 2,000 years ago, as mankind languished in sin, God put on a face and sent His only Son to earth as a newborn baby, just a few miles down the road from Jerusalem.

Yet, Jesus was around long before that. As we examine the Son, let's start with His **inception.** As the second member of the Trinity, Jesus existed before the world began. Scripture says, *"In the beginning was the Word, and the Word was with God and the **Word was God"** (John 1:1, emphasis added).

Note the portion of the verse that I put in bold letters. Why? Because Jesus is God! Teaching in the temple, Jesus proclaimed, *"I and the Father are one."* A few days later, he said to the disciples, *"He who has seen Me has seen the Father"* (John 10:30, 14:9). Paul clearly supports these claims, writing *"He is the image of the invisible God, the firstborn of* all creation. For in Him all the fullness of Deity exists in bodily form" (Colossians 1:15, 2:9).

I never tire of stressing this vital truth. It's what separates Christianity from all other cults and false faiths proliferating around us. Many other religions and "isms" throughout the globe acknowledge the existence of Jesus. They even endorse Him as an effective prophet and teacher. Yet, they deny His Deity, rejecting Him as the only path to salvation.

And since there's never been a time when He wasn't, it is evident Jesus assisted in creation. As the Bible states: *"All things came into being through Him, and apart from Him nothing came into being that has come into being"* (John 1:3).

ETERNITY INVADES TIME

Let us now speak of **incarnation,** that pivotal point where eternity invaded time and Jesus became one of us. But instead of heading back *to* Bethlehem, let's go back *before* Bethlehem.

As "The Angel of the LORD," Christ made numerous pre-incarnate appearances in the Old Testament. The first of these Christophanies as they're called, took place in the wilderness of Shur after the maidservant Hagar received harsh treatment from Abram's wife Sarai and fled the house (Genesis 16; 7-15). Perhaps the most notable examples took place when Jacob wrestled "a man" for a blessing (Genesis 32:24-32), the "Angel of the LORD" appeared to Moses in a burning bush (Exodus 3:1-6), and the "son of the gods," the fourth man who protected Shadrach, Meshach, and Abednego from the fiery furnace (Daniel 3:19-30).

Digging deeper into this discussion of Christ's incarnation, carefully consider these three key characteristics related to it:

Humble servant—Although Jesus is God, He *"did not regard equality with God a thing to be grasped, but emptied Himself, taking the form* *of a bond servant"* (Philippians 2:6,7). He willingly left a blissful heaven, coming to Satan's domain, this sin-stained earth. Instead of insisting on and clinging to the privileges of eternal deity, He sacrificed that status, entering temporal time in *"the form of a bond-servant."* Everything about His earthly existence—birth, life, and death— exhibited humility.

Virgin birth—The virgin birth of Christ, a monumental Kingdom axiom, is "anticipated in Genesis (3:15), prophesied in Isaiah (7:14), and proclaimed in Matthew and Luke."[1]

When Mary asked Gabriel how this could happen since she was a virgin, the angel Gabriel answered, *"The Holy Spirit will come upon you, and the power of the most high will overshadow you"* (Luke 1:35). God had to be the Father, for otherwise Jesus would have had the blood of a sinful Adam flowing through His veins, thus rendering His sacrifice for sin unacceptable.

Fully human—Speaking of Jesus, the Bible says, *"The Word became flesh, and dwelt among us"* (John 1:14). Paul states that He was *"made in the likeness of men"* (Philippians 2:7).

As I've already alluded, Jesus did not cease being God when He became a man. He was the "God-Man." In fact, his favorite designation for Himself was "Son of Man" —a title He used 87 times.

He was a Jew, raised in a Jewish home. Attending the synagogue in Nazareth, He studied what we now call the Old Testament. Being human, He faced temptations like the rest of us –the difference being, He never sinned. He experienced hunger and thirst, shed tears, and expressed joy and compassion, which leads nicely into the next section, a brief description of Jesus' **earthly ministry.**

During this three-year time, which the Gospels carefully record, Jesus engaged primarily in a three-fold ministry of preaching, teaching, and healing. He fed the hungry, raised the dead, led the lame to walk and restored sight to the blind. He played no favorites, spending time with the up-and-comers, the down-and-outs, and everyone in between. Rather than pointing fingers and berating the sinful, He lovingly exposed their transgressions, directing them to a better way in life.

In a time in history and society when true mentors and heroes are difficult to find, look no further than Jesus Christ. The night before His crucifixion, after washing the disciples' feet, Jesus said, *"I gave you an example that you should do as I did to you"* (John 13:15). Mother Teresa, the Catholic nun who spent most of her adult life in India ministering to the poorest of the poor, faithfully followed Jesus' lead.

> On one occasion she was brought face to face with a man who had a rare and horrendous case of terminal cancer. One of the workers had vomited from the stench and could no longer continue. Mother Teresa then stepped in and kindly took over. The patient was mystified. "How can you stand the smell?" asked the patient. Mother Teresa replied, "It's nothing compared to the pain you must feel." Servanthood begins when we move beyond our own comfort to relieve the discomfort of another.[2]

One of the disciples present on that night before the crucifixion, writing about the example Christ displayed, challenges readers to: *"follow in His steps"* (1 Peter 2:21). May the chorus to the old hymn serve as our mantra: "Footprints of Jesus that make the pathway glow; we will follow the steps of Jesus wher-e'er they go."[3]

Although most people who encountered Jesus left better off, many becoming faithful followers, a few rejected and hated Him. Among them was the religious establishment, some who conspired to kill Jesus from the beginning of His public work (Mark 3:6).

Ultimately, it wasn't an earthly plot that put Jesus on the cross, but rather an eternal plan. As John states in the last book of the Bible, He was *"The Lamb slain from the foundation of the world"* (Revelation 13:8, KJV). Carefully consider the following description of Jesus' **death.** It was:

Violent—As intense and excessive as most Hollywood movies are, they don't fully capture the horrific scenes depicting Christ's final hours. Beaten with a whip that had pieces of bone and metal on the end *"his appearance was so disfigured beyond that of any man and his form marred beyond human likeness"* (Isaiah 52:14).

After that, Jesus was forced to carry his own cross, an inhuman instrument of death that makes hanging, the electric chair, firing squad, and lethal injection seem mild in comparison.

With nails through His hands and feet, Jesus hung in excruciating pain for hours.

Vital—The society in which we live may tolerate and propagate sin, but make no mistake about it, God hates it. He despises sin so much that He can't even look at it (Habakkuk 1:13). Our transgressions are such an abomination that the sacrifice of animals can't touch them. It took the death of His only Son to pay the ransom and save us from an eternity in Hell.

Because of His pierced body, we have been redeemed, bought back from being a slave to sin. Thanks to His shed blood, we have been justified, our records have been cleared, our slates have been wiped clean. *"As far as the east is from the west, so far has He removed our transgressions from us"* (Psalm 103:12).

Vicarious—It should have been you and me on that cross. Instead, it was the only perfect man that ever lived.

One of my favorite children's books is Sid Fleischman's Newbery medal-winning *The Whipping Boy*. One of the main characters is Horace, spoiled son of the King, nicknamed "Prince Brat." Though constantly misbehaving, Horace can't be disciplined because no one is to place a hand on the prince. Therefore, a poor orphaned boy becomes "the whipping boy," beaten several times a day for the Prince's wrongdoing. Jesus, the supreme whipping boy, not only took the whipping, He ultimately died on our behalf.

Voluntary—Earlier, I mentioned that angry Jews plotted to kill Jesus. They even tried to push Him over a cliff after He preached in

His hometown of Nazareth (Luke 4:29). Such attempts were unsuccessful because the timing was not right. His death would go according to God's timing and terms.

GIVEN NOT TAKEN

Early in His ministry Jesus proclaimed, *"As Moses lifted up the serpent in the wilderness* (Numbers 21:5-9), *even so must the Son of Man be lifted up"* (John 3:14). This crisis for the Hebrews en route to the Promised Land symbolized Christ's being lifted on a Cross centuries later. And when that time came, Jesus willingly submitted. Referring to His life, Jesus later said, *"No one takes it from Me, but I lay it down on My own initiative. For even the Son of Man did not come to be served, but to serve, and to give His life a ransom for many"* (John 10:18, Mark 10:45).

Victorious—Scripture details some wonderful victories. Joshua led God's army against Jericho, as the walls crumbled before them. Young David felled the giant Goliath with a single shot to the forehead. After the Tribulation, the Lord will return to the earth, leading a heavenly army to defeat God's enemies (Revelation 19:11-16, 19-21).

Yet none of these conquests, or any other throughout history for that matter, can compare to Christ's ultimate victory at Calvary. Jesus' heel was bruised on that day, but Satan's head was crushed (Genesis 3:15). The Lord's cry of *"It is finished"* (John 19:30) meant death, the devil, and sin had been defeated.

Jesus died on that apex in history 2,000 years ago, but thankfully, just three days later His **resurrection** followed the crucifixion. Discovering an empty tomb when they checked on the gravesite, His followers heard from angels present that first Easter morning, *"He is not here; he has risen"* (Luke 24:6).

After the 1917 Bolshevik revolution, the local communist leader had been sent to a Russian village to tell the people the virtues of communism and to take their minds away from religion, which Karl Marx called "the opium of the people."

After the communist, had harangued them for a long time, he said to the local Christian pastor rather hatefully: "I will give you five minutes to reply."

The pastor replied: "I do not need five minutes, only five seconds." He rose to the platform and gave the Easter greeting: "The Lord is risen!" As one man the villagers thundered back: "He is risen indeed!"

If Christ had not been raised, our preaching would be pointless and our faith futile. Death would reign supreme and we'd still be lost in our sin.

The fact is, He not only experienced resurrection, but **ascension** as well.

CHRIST'S WORK CONTINUES

Forty days after rising forth from the grave, following numerous resurrection appearances to individuals and crowds, Jesus transported from the Mount of Olives outside Jerusalem to His rightful place and present location at the right hand of the Father in Heaven. Christ's ascension set many Kingdom occurrences in motion, two of which I'd like to focus upon.

The Holy Spirit descended—The Lord told His disciples, *"it is to your advantage that I go away . . . if I go, I will send Him, to you"* (John 16:7). Ten days later, the Spirit, the third member of the Trinity, came, and the church emerged. An entire chapter on the Holy Spirit is coming up.

Christ continues His work—Jesus isn't sitting on a cloud playing a harp. He continues to minister, *interceding* on our behalf before the Father (Romans 8:34, Hebrews 7:25). Just as the High

Priest appeared before God on behalf of the Hebrews, pleading forgiveness for their sins, Jesus perpetually stands before the Father, serving as our defense attorney. He mediates on our behalf, providing assurance that our sins have been forgiven and paid for.

Once while lecturing before Princeton University, theologian Karl Barth was asked, "Sir, don't you think God has revealed Himself in other religions and not only Christianity?" Barth thundered back, "No, God has not revealed Himself in any religion, including Christianity. He has revealed Himself in His Son."

I hope His Son has been revealed more clearly to you through the words in this chapter. Let's move now and see what necessitated His coming to earth.

4

PARADISE POSTPONED

"Therefore the Lord God sent him out
from the Garden of Eden"
(Genesis 3:23).

෨෬

Back in the turbulent late 60s/early 70s, legendary singer/songwriter Joni Mitchell escaped smog-blanketed Los Angeles for a first time visit to Hawaii. Standing on her high-rise hotel room balcony, Joni gazed at the post card beauty of swaying palm trees and the blue Pacific. Suddenly, her mood changed when she looked down and spotted an ugly, concrete parking garage on the hotel grounds. She thought, "They paved paradise and put up a parking lot." Seizing the moment, the resourceful artist parlayed these words into the mega-hit "Big Yellow Taxi." Nearly four decades later, the song not only survives, but thrives.

Several millennia prior, Adam and Eve must have pondered similar thoughts while the bitter aftertaste of forbidden fruit lingered on their tongues. In response to their disobedience, God banished them from the Garden and forced them to maintain sustenance by the sweat of their brows. They exchanged the paradise of Eden for a life of physical pain and toil. Yet such punishment pales in comparison to an infinitely more severe sentence, the influx of sin and alienation from God.

How could God's plan have taken such a turn? One might say it all began when the serpent—or devil in disguise—approached and questioned Eve on that infamous day. However, this earthly encounter had its roots in a previous, heavenly battle. Satan was once a prominent angelic servant of God. Named Lucifer, or "shining one," he was the "light bearer." "He had no natural light of his own but was expected to reflect the light and glory of God."[1]

Describing this privileged messenger, the prophet Ezekiel said, *"You were anointed as a guardian cherub, for so I ordained you. You were on the holy mount of God; you walked among the fiery stones. You were blameless in your ways from the day you were created **till wickedness was found in you**"* (Ezekiel 28:14,15, emphasis added).

As "guardian cherub," Lucifer conducted and orchestrated the worship of other angels. "He received the worship of the angels beneath him and passed it on to God above him. None of the adoration was to be diverted along the way. God alone deserved all that was accorded Him."[2]

And yet, that all changed when wickedness reared its ugly head and ruined a previously perfect being. Arrogance took control. Full of himself, Lucifer boasted, *"I will raise my throne above the stars of God . . . I will make myself **like the Most High**"* (Isaiah 14:13,14, emphasis added).

What prompted such pride? Milton believes that the creation of Adam and Eve caused Lucifer to be mastered by intense jealousy, and that his sin came in the wake of their formation.[3] After all, they were created in God's image and had the capability of fellowship with Him that angels did not enjoy. Whatever the cause, he placed self-interest ahead of God-interest. Because he sought to take what rightfully belonged to his Creator, Lucifer was kicked out of heaven and *"cast* down to the earth" (Isaiah 14:12) —along with a host of fallen angels who sided with him.

SATAN'S PLOY

Left to rehash and, I believe, regret his decision, Lucifer, now Satan, waited until another devilish opportunity surfaced. The timing and method of his madness were critical. Unwilling to pass up an opportunity to inflict upon God's prized creation the pain he had brought upon himself, the adversary resorted to **deception**.

He could have obnoxiously accosted Eve, spewing fury, but that would have certainly tipped his hand. Instead, he inhabited the body of a serpent and implemented a cunning approach. Pre-Fall circumstances help explain why Eve remained with fascination rather than flee in fear. In addition, this was surely a beautiful creature, not the repulsive reptile that slithers along the ground.

Satan's strategy involves masking intentions, downplaying consequences, and masquerading himself as an *"angel of light"* (2 Corinthians 11:14), not unlike the Jehovah's Witness who came to my door a few years ago. Armed with slick color literature, a polite smile, and a sweet child by his side, he didn't begin the conversation by asking, "Could I interest you in some false doctrine this afternoon?" Yet, a closer look at the Watchtower Society faith statement reveals a salvation based on works, a denial of the Deity of Jesus Christ, and the belief that no human soul exists after death.

Paul warned the church at Corinth, *"But I am afraid that just as Eve was deceived by the serpent's cunning, your minds may somehow be led astray from your sincere and pure devotion to Christ. For if someone comes to you and preaches a Jesus other than the Jesus we preached, or if you receive a different spirit from the one you received, or a different gospel from the one you accepted, you put up with it easily enough"* (2 Corinthians 11:4).

Satan peddles a gospel that provides temporal gratification instead of eternal regeneration—one that places the focus on creature rather than Creator. Most of the time he concocts a palatable blend of truth and error. When the situation demands it, however, he resorts to blatant lies. In fact, Jesus called him *"a liar and the father of lies"* (John 8:44).

He told his first lie in the garden, assuring Eve that she would "not surely die" when she ate the forbidden fruit. Thus, they partook, and the Devil got caught in a lie. "They did die on the day they ate. Their bodies began to die *physically*; their deterioration would be slow but inevitable. They died *spiritually,* in that they were separated from God. They would also die *eternally* unless God were to intervene."[4]

As effective as it was, deception was not the only arrow Satan pulled from the quiver on that day of destruction. He also introduced **doubt**, resorting to an attack on the very words of God. He asked, *"Did God really say, 'You must not eat from any tree in the garden'?"* (Genesis 3:1). In other words, "How do you know those were the words of God? Are you certain of their meaning? After all, you weren't even there when they were spoken." Eve loosely paraphrased the words of God (compare Genesis 2:16,17 with 3:2,3), a move that no doubt emboldened the serpent.

Satan continued to feed Eve's insecurity by leading her to believe that God was deceiving and keeping something good from her and her husband. He said, *"For God knows that when you eat of it your eyes will be opened, and you will be like God, knowing good and evil"* (Genesis 3:5). Observe the adversary's strategy. Rather than allude to the hundreds of beautiful trees available to them, the Devil steered Eve toward the only one off limits, a tactic he continues to use. Satan knows that if he can get us to focus on the one thing we lack, he can steal any joy derived from what we do have.

Eve became the first, but certainly not the last, to fall victim to this scheme. Clouded and confused by Satan's deception and doubt, she was overcome by **desire**. When Eve *"saw that the fruit of the tree* *was good for food and pleasing to the eye, and also desirable for gaining wisdom, she took some and ate it. She also gave some to her husband, who was with her, and he ate it"* (Genesis 3:6).

Flush with land, money, talent, the respect of his subjects, and, best of all, the anointing of God, King David looked from the palace roof and spotted one of the few things that didn't belong to him: Bathsheba—the beautiful wife of one of his soldiers. Abusing his power, he committed adultery and arranged for the murder of her husband. And though he sought and received God's forgiveness, this episode certainly contributed to the dysfunction in his family.

Like David, Adam and Eve were surrounded by a sea of yeses but still chose no. They had everything and then lost it by letting Satan con them into perpetrating the one act God forbade. This one bad tree propagated into a dense forest that served to alienate man from God – separate but not sever.

GOD'S RESPONSE

Like the crucifixion that came several millennia later, this dark hour in the Garden did not catch God by surprise. And rather than turn away from the crown jewel of creation, He tracked Adam and Eve down and implemented His punishment and plan.

Notice God's **curses**, the first of which He inflicted upon the serpent. *"Cursed are you above all the livestock and all the wild animals! You will crawl on your belly and you will eat dust all the days of your life"* (Genesis 3:14). The creature had lent its body to the evil one and must then pay the price.

God then established animosity between the serpent and the woman, a gulf that would extend into their respective offspring. Eventually in the lineage, as we'll discover in later chapters, a male child appears that strikes a death blow to the serpent – *"he will crush your head, and you will strike his heel"* (Genesis 3:15).

God also plagued the earth by stating, *"Cursed is the ground because of you. It will produce thorns and thistles for you"* (Genesis 3:17,18). Paul elaborated on the earth's fall when he informed the church at Rome: *"The creation was subjected to frustration, not only by its own choice, but by the will of the one who subjected it"* (Romans 8:20). I believe this includes such natural disasters as hurricanes, floods and earthquakes, as well as the steady decay process to which the earth has been subjected.

The key recipients of the curse, however, were Adam, Eve, and their descendants —the billions in which you and I are included. As previously mentioned, God reacted to their rebellion by initiating the death process –both physical and spiritual. And in addition to forcing Adam into hard labor upon the sin-saturated earth, God dealt with Eve by greatly increasing the pain during her childbearing.

Note, too, the Lord said, *"Man has now become like one of us, knowing good and evil. He must not be allowed to reach out his hand and take also from the tree of life and eat, and live forever"* (Genesis 3:22). To help solidify this sentence, God banished Adam and Eve from Eden and then placed an armed angel on its east side to keep them from getting back in.

Ironically, this part of the curse set the stage for **correction**, because, if the couple had eaten of the tree of life in their fallen condition, they would have remained forever in their sins. "They would have become like the fallen angels, incapable of death and forever locked into the guilt and penalty of their sin. It would have become impossible to renew them to repentance."[5]

Garments of skin were also included in this process of restoration and redemption. Once Adam and Eve's eyes were opened and the couple experienced guilt for the first time, they covered themselves with fig leaves. This attempt proved futile, because they couldn't do for themselves what only God could provide. A contribution from a plant could never compare to the sacrifice of an animal. The necessity of blood and death in sacrifice is underscored later when God rejected Cain's offering from the soil and accepted Abel's fat portions from his flock (Genesis 4:3-5). Both instances, of course, point toward Jesus' provision of blood and loss of life at Calvary.

"WHERE ARE YOU?"

I must now ask the question posed to the man on that fateful day in the garden, *"Where are you?"* (Genesis 3:9). Are you modeling Adam by sewing fig leaves together, fabricating a shallow, temporary cover-up for guilt and shame? That's an extremely risky venture, since the Bible says, *"In Adam all die."* The good news is, the second half of that verse promises that, *"In Christ, all will be made alive"* (1 Corinthians 15:22). We are made alive by the freedom and covering that only His blood provides. As Scripture confirms, *"If we walk in the light, as he is in the light, we have fellowship with one another, and the blood of Jesus, his son, purifies us from all sin"* (1 John 1:7).

I once picked up a magazine at a local health club that described how I could locate and purchase my own little piece of paradise. I probed further to discover Bottle Cay in the Bahamas, a gorgeous, ten-acre island complete with cottage, rainwater well, and windmill—all for a mere $800,000.[6]

Just like Adam and Eve before the fall, I plan to enjoy real paradise someday. Only it'll be much bigger than a few measly acres, void of concrete parking lots, and it won't cost a thing. God already paid for it, as you'll discover more clearly in the next chapter to come.

Todd Gaddis

5

3:16 TO ETERNITY

"For God so loved the world . . ."
(John 3:16).

෯෬෯

3 :10 to Yuma, a 2007 movie remake based on a short story by Elmore Leonard, ranks as one of Hollywood's best Westerns in recent years. In this Academy Award nominated film, Russell Crowe plays a notorious outlaw named Ben Wade, who robs an armored stagecoach and is soon arrested in an Arizona saloon. He is then turned over to a convoy who agree to take him to a town called Contention, where he will be put on the 3:10 train to the Yuma Territorial Prison—thus the title.

Although "3:10" symbolizes a criminal's journey to incarceration, the numbers in this opening section, 3:16, reveal a sinner's hope for freedom. As Jesus said, *"For God so loved the world that he gave his one and only Son, that whoever believes in him shall not perish but have eternal life"* (John 3:16).

"YOU MUST BE BORN AGAIN"

Our story begins when a high-ranking Jewish religious leader named Nicodemus recognizes the power of God in Jesus and comes to Him for answers. At the outset of the conversation, the Lord declared, *"I tell you the truth no one can see the kingdom of God unless he is born again"* (John 3:3).

This phrase, "born again," has taken a beating from the secular media, but as you can see, it's absolutely biblical. Our first birth, being born of the flesh, takes place when we emerge from our mother's womb. Our second birth, which comes from the Spirit, occurs when we receive Jesus as our Savior and thus become citizens of God's kingdom.

In the winter of 1982, I was working as a salesman in the agricultural chemical field. One night while on the road, I opened the motel phone drawer and found an evangelistic tract titled, *"Are You Born Again?"* I believed I was. I had grown up in church, been baptized as a child, and attended regularly my entire young life. As I read through this gospel presentation, however, conviction closed in. I came to realize that I needed a personal relationship with Christ. I understood that belief and repentance, rather than ritual and religiosity, trigger a person's conversion experience.

To get this point across to Nicodemus, Jesus unveiled humanity's perilous predicament, **our need for God's love**. He connected with the Pharisee's Jewish Hebrew heritage by referring to an incident that took place as the children of Israel traveled from Egypt to Canaan. Responding to the Israelite's complaint about meager food and lack of water, God sent venomous snakes among the people, which bit and killed many. The Lord then said to Moses, *"Make a snake and put it on a pole; anyone who is bitten can look at it and live"* (Numbers 21:8). So, Moses made a bronze snake, which the people looked upon and lived.

In the same manner as the rebellious Jews were bitten by venomous snakes, we've all been bitten by the poison of sin. Church attendance, baptism and good deeds are important, yet the only antidote for this deadly condition is the Son of Man, Jesus Christ Himself, being lifted up and crucified on the cross.

With that in mind, note that God responded to our sinful state with **His gift of love**. Scripture says, *"For God so loved the world that he gave"* (John 3:16, emphasis added). Jesus' sacrifice was a demonstration of absolute grace and mercy. We did nothing to earn this gift and we certainly didn't deserve it.

Jesus later confirmed this truth, saying, *"The reason my Father loves me is that I lay down my life—only to take it up again"* (John 10:17). He was not forced to go to the cross. No one *took* His life. Jesus *gave* it because of His unconditional love for us. John, in his first epistle, builds further on this monumental event: *"This is how we know what love is: Jesus Christ laid down his life for us"* (1 John 3:16).

SUFFERING LOVE

Although it's not specifically described in these verses, it is important to grasp **the suffering involved in this exhibition of love**. Speaking to the disciples and referring to Himself, Jesus said that the Son of man, love incarnate, *"must suffer many things"* (Mark 8:31). He is the Lamb of God *"that was slain from the creation of the world"* (Revelation 13:8).

One of the main words I would use to describe Mel Gibson's 2004 blockbuster movie, *The Passion of the Christ* is bloody. Some might think, in typical Hollywood fashion, it was sensationalized. Yet the Bible says: *"Without the shedding of blood there is no forgiveness"* (Hebrews 9:22). Referring to Jesus' beating and crucifixion, the Bible says that *"His appearance was so disfigured beyond that of any man and his form marred beyond human likeness"* (Isaiah 52:14).

Bleeding Love, performed by British artist Leona Lewis, is among the top singles of the 21st century. Written by Jesse McCartney and

Ryan Tedder, it was the #1 worldwide hit in 2008. As you might guess, this tune tells the story of a heartsick person who wears scars and bleeds love over a severed relationship. It's a powerful song, yet pales in comparison to the bleeding love that flowed down Calvary's Cross outside Jerusalem 2000 years ago. Still wearing the scars, Jesus strongly desires that our relationship with Him would be fruitful. We must do our part, however, and willingly come to Him.

As believers, we should anticipate this love/suffering connection taking place in our lives as well. Loving means exposing ourselves to suffering. In fact, those we love sometimes hurt us the most, and vice versa. Those we dearly love sometime slap us in the face, kick us in the teeth, and punch us in the gut—figuratively speaking. God's Son received far worse and yet He poured out His love in even greater measure.

From John 3:16 we also see the **inclusive range of God's love.** Jesus said that *"whoever believes in him shall not perish"* (John 3:16, emphasis added). The Gospel is accessible to all who believe, regardless of gender, race, nationality, age, economic status, etc.

God used a dream to help Peter overcome his resistance to Gentiles becoming believers. In this vision, the apostle saw a sheet full of "unclean" animals and was instructed by God to eat from them. Grasping the truth from the dream, Peter later said to a Gentile named Cornelius: *"I now realize how true it is that God does not show favoritism but accepts men from every nation who fear him and do what is right"* (Acts 10:34,35). He later wrote in one of his epistles that the Lord does not want *"anyone to perish, but everyone to come to repentance"* (2 Peter 3:9). Paul said, *"God . . . wants **all** men to be saved and to come to a knowledge of the truth"* (1 Timothy 2:3-4, emphasis added).

My local gym has a notice posted at the entrance that reads: STOP (THIS FITNESS CLUB) IS A MEMBERS ONLY FACILITY. Similarly, I've seen plenty of signs on doors inside large retail establishments that say: "Do not enter, employees only beyond this point." Such is not the case when it comes to entrance into the kingdom of God. Scripture promises, *"Everyone who calls on the name of the Lord will be saved"* (Romans 10:13); or as the chorus to the old J. Edwin McConnell hymn says "Whosoever meaneth me."

In addition to God's limited love, John 3:16 describes the following **privileges resulting from God's love.**

Eternal life—Those who come to Christ, *"Shall not perish but have eternal life"* (John 3:16). Is Jesus saying that Christians will avoid physical death, like Enoch and Elijah of the Old Testament? No, because *"Man is destined to die **once**"* (Hebrews 9:27, emphasis added). Our bodies are in the process of deteriorating, and unless the Lord returns first, we're headed for an earthly grave.

But that doesn't mean we must die twice. Tragically, the unbelieving who fail to convert will be thrown into the lake of fire following Jesus' Second Coming and millennial reign (more on these subjects later). God's Word calls this *"the second death"* (Revelation 2:14). As the little saying goes, "born twice-die once, born once-die twice."

Imagine the never-ending joy of the presence of the Lord, His saints and angels—no more pain, sin, suffering or death. Nothing in this life can compare. Nothing on this planet remotely equates to the bliss and beauty of the new heaven and new earth that await believers at the end times. Yet, as great as all this will be, please understand that receiving Jesus Christ involves so much more than a rescue from hell. Salvation, which guarantees eternal life, also provides for:

Abundant life—I run across far too many anxiety-ridden, doom and gloom Christians who look as though they just took a big swig of pickle juice. They sing of one day crossing Jordan's stormy banks into the Promised Land, but in the meantime, they'll grunt and grumble their way through this earthly life, missing out on the best God has to offer.

Jesus proclaimed, *"I am come that they might have life, and that they might have it more abundantly"* (John 10:10, KJV). On a previous occasion, He said, *"Whoever believes in me . . . streams of living water will flow from within him"* (John 7:38) Streams of living water refer to the presence of the Holy Spirit in the life of a born-again believer — waters which allow for joy, not only in the sweet by and by, but in the blessed here and now as well.

If you claim to be a Christian and yet would not describe your life as peaceful and fulfilling, something is not right. Certainly, you're going to face periods of discouragement and difficulty, yet that should not be your permanent state of mind.

God's will for your life is that you experience a spiritually bountiful life.

This desire is far more likely to become reality as **you continually seek to keep your love relationship with Christ pure and fulfilling**—the key to which can be found in Jesus' closing comment to Nicodemus: *"But whoever lives by the truth comes into the light, so that it may be seen plainly that what he has done has been done through God"* (John 3:21). Note these concluding commands:

Come into the light—Those seeking the truth gravitate to light. For example, consider the account in the Christmas story where the wise men came to Jesus bearing gifts of gold, incense, and myrrh. After Christ was born, a star shone above Bethlehem that guided the Magi to the King of Kings and Lord of Lords. They saw the light and came to Him.

Fittingly, Jesus later referred to Himself as *"The light of the world."* He added: *"Whoever follows me will never walk in darkness, but will have the light of life"* (John 8:12). Yet recognizing the light and walking in it is only part of the spiritual equation. We must also:

Reflect that light to others—According to our passage, we come to the light, seeking truth, *"So that it may be seen plainly that what* (we have) *done has been done through God"* (John 3:21). A kingdom paradox surfaces here. Obviously, we aren't to perform good deeds in order to be noticed by others. We are no doubt commanded, however, to give evidence of the love and work of God in our lives.

As the Lord said, *"Let your light shine before men, so that they may see your good deeds"* (Matthew 5:16).

The defining issue is motive. Our works become tainted when we do them in order to gain attention and glory for ourselves. However, a sweet fragrance goes forth when our sole desire is that God gets the glory. As Jesus said, *"Let your light shine before men, so that they may see your good deeds* **and praise your Father in heaven**" (Matthew 5:16, emphasis added).

An article appearing in *National Geographic* years ago provides a penetrating picture of God's sacrificial love. Following a forest fire in Yellowstone National Park, rangers began to trek up a mountain to assess the damage. One member of the party found a bird petrified in ashes, statuesquely perched on the ground at the base of a tree. Sickened by the sight, he knocked the bird over with a stick. Suddenly, three tiny chicks scurried from under their dead mother's wings. Keenly aware of the coming danger, the loving mother carried her babies to the base of the tree and protected them under her wings. She could have flown to safety but chose to die for her offspring instead.[1]

A heartless, abstract god might have abandoned his creation to continual hopelessness under the poisonous spell of sin. However, as John 3:16 so passionately describes, our loving Father chose to send His only Son to die in our place so that we might find forgiveness for sin and receive eternal life.

Before advancing to the next chapter, make sure you realize the absolute need we all have for God's love. If you haven't before, receive this free gift, understanding the suffering involved in bringing it about. Remember, this matchless love that is available to all, results in abundant and eternal life. Embrace the Father's offer by coming to Him and going to others.

Todd Gaddis

6

"THE MUSIC IS IN ME"

"It is no longer I who live, but Christ lives in me"
(Galatians 2:20).

∞൦രൠ

Nicolo Paganini (1782-1840), one of the greatest violinists of all time, was about to perform before a sold-out opera house. Walking on stage to a huge ovation, he sensed something wrong. He realized that he had someone else's violin in his hands. Terrified, but knowing that he had no other choice, he began.

He gave the performance of his life that evening. After the concert, talking with another musician, he admitted, "Today I learned the most important lesson of my entire career. Before today I thought the music was in the violin; today I learned that the music is in me."

Next to Christ as Savior, the best discovery I've ever made was that I had the "music in me"—that is the presence and power of the Holy Spirit. The Biblical term for this is **baptism** of the Spirit. John the Baptist arrived on the scene preaching, "*I baptize you with water for repentance, but He who is coming after me...will baptize you with the Holy Spirit and fire*" (Matthew 3:11). Although some branches of the

41

Christian faith teach otherwise, I believe this baptism is synonymous with salvation itself.

Paul addressed this subject often, likening the Holy Spirit to both a seal and deposit. As He said, *"Having also believed, you were **sealed** in Him with the Holy Spirit of promise"* (Ephesians 1:13, emphasis added)." At this time, God *"anointed us . . . and put his Spirit in our hearts as a **deposit**, guaranteeing what is to come"* (2 Corinthians 1:21-22, emphasis added). The seal indicates God's authentication and ownership on our lives, whereas the deposit is a pledge in the present that God will bring our salvation to fruition, award us our future inheritance in Christ, and see that we spend eternity in His presence.

A HE, NOT AN IT

The Bible says, *"If anyone does not have the Spirit of Christ, he does not belong to Christ. The Spirit **Himself** testifies with our spirit that we are children of God"* (Romans 8:9,16, emphasis added). Note carefully the bold faced personal pronoun in that verse. The Holy Spirit is not an it but a Person, a He in fact. "Himself" is capitalized because the Spirit is God, the third member of the Trinity. Possessing all the attributes of God, not only did He participate in creation (Gen 1:2), He's absolutely vital to the regeneration process as well (John 3:5,6, Titus 3:5,6).

But since we've already discussed much of this, I want to focus on these additional roles unique to the Holy Spirit. Not only does the Spirit baptize, He also **produces** the following in every believer:

Fruit—Jesus proclaimed in the Sermon on the Mount, *"You will know them by their fruits. So every good tree bears good fruit, but the bad tree bears bad fruit"* (Matthew 7:16,17). *"My Father is glorified by this; that you bear much fruit, and so prove to be My disciples,"* He said the night before His death (John 15:8).

What fruit should a believer bear? Paul provides this brief, yet comprehensive list: *"But the fruit of the Spirit is love, joy, peace, patience, kindness, goodness, faithfulness, gentleness, self-control."* (Galatians 5:22,23). While this verse is representative of that which we should bear, it's not exhaustive. Certainly, the best fruit a Christian can help bring forth is the birth of a new believer.

If I plant a tomato seedling, I'm satisfied with green stems and leaves for a while, but eventually I expect to see some tasty, red fruit. Likewise, as God's children, we must produce fruit as a result of the Spirit in us.

Gifts—All believers should strive to produce as much and as many kinds of fruit as possible. However, gifts are a different matter. Simply explained, these gifts are "Spirit-given abilities for Christian service."[1] Every believer receives at least one, perhaps more, at the point of conversion. And though interpretations vary, I believe God's Word reveals 19 gifts. Note in the table below that 18 of the 19 appear in three different epistles written by Paul. Peter includes the final gift, *hospitality* (1 Peter 4:9,10).

Romans 12:3-8	1 Corinthians 12:8-10, 28-30		Ephesians 4:11
Prophecy	Wisdom	Tongues	Apostleship
Service	Knowledge	Interpretation	Prophecy
Teaching	Faith	Apostleship	Evangelism
Encouraging	Healing	Teaching	Pastoring
Giving	Miracles	Service	Teaching
Administration	Prophecy	Administration	
Mercy	Discernment		

To reiterate, understand that gifts are *divinely granted*. As the Bible says, *"one and the same Spirit works all these things, distributing to each one individually just as He wills"* (1 Corinthians 12:11). These gifts *necessarily diversified*. If you were a gigantic ear, imagine how well you could hear. Yet you wouldn't be able to see, touch, taste, or smell. In the same way, the Spirit distributes gifts in the body of Christ so we can all contribute in different ways. These gifts should be *diligently desired.* As Scripture says, *"Pursue love, yet desire earnestly spiritual gifts"* (1 Corinthians 14:1). We should not compare ourselves to others and covet what God has given them. Rather, we must mine deeply into our own soul and spirit to discover and relish what the Spirit has bestowed upon us. Finally, these gifts must be *carefully maintained.* These directives from Paul provide further insight: *"Do not neglect the spiritual gift within you. Kindle afresh the gift of God which is in you . . ."* (1 Timothy 4:14, 2 Timothy 1:6). Though the Holy Spirit gave them to us, He's not going to develop and maintain them for us. He does His part and we must do ours, experimenting with and implementing them at every opportunity.

In chapter two we discussed that the Son *reveals*, whereas the Holy Spirit *executes*. Nowhere is this more evident than in His role as a **guide.** Jesus said, on the night before His crucifixion, *"When He, the Spirit of truth comes, He will guide you into all the truth"* (John 16:13). Note these specific ways the Spirit guides.

He convicts—Perhaps you've heard about the man who felt guilty because He cheated on his taxes. After months of sleepless nights, He sent a check for $1,000 to the IRS with a short note enclosed. "If, after sending you this $1,000, I still feel guilty, I'll mail in the rest of what I owe."

Chances are the Holy Spirit was working in that man's life. As the Bible says, the Spirit convicts *"the world concerning sin and righteousness and judgment"* (John 16:8). In order for a person to be saved, they must first realize they are lost. It is the Spirit's job to expose their sin and convince them of their need for a Savior. Conscience alone can't accomplish that. Once saved, we have Him living in us to continue the conviction process and direct us toward confession.

He teaches—Jesus is the greatest teacher in the history of the world, but He is no longer here. Upon ascending, He passed that job along to the third member of the Trinity. According to Jesus, *"He will teach you all things and bring to your remembrance all that I said to you"* (John 14:26).

This 2,000-year legacy continues as, through the tutelage of the Holy Spirit, we blessedly receive the teachings of Jesus. My preaching would be flat and ineffective were it not for the Spirit's anointing and amplification. Whether you're teaching others or learning for yourself, pray earnestly that the Holy Spirit would provide inspiration and clarification as you study.

He counsels—The Greek word used for this role, "paraclete," is rendered Counselor, Comforter, or Helper, depending on the translation. "It is used as 'one who stands alongside' as a lawyer, particularly for the defense."[2]

"Wait a minute Preacher," one might question, "didn't you say in Chapter 3 that Jesus was the one doing that?" In a sense, yes. He is also referred to as a paraclete, yet His role is different. "He (Jesus) is the Christian's advocate with God, pleading his case before God; the Holy Spirit is God's advocate, pleading His case before our hearts."[3] How magnificent it is that the Holy Spirit can both instruct the mind of the seeker and console the heart of the sorrowful.

He calls and sends—Isaiah said: *"Come near me and listen to this: The Sovereign Lord has sent me, with his Spirit"* (Isaiah 48:16). The prophet's task of going before a rebellious and disobedient people would be impossible to accomplish were it not for divine marching orders. And even in this Old Testament period when the Holy Spirit was not yet permanently residing *within* God's people, the third Person of the Godhead gave strength to carry out the job.

Centuries later, after the coming of Christ and the birth of the church, *"The Holy Spirit said, 'Set apart for me Barnabas and Saul for the work to which I have called them ....' The two of them, sent on their way by the Holy Spirit . . ."* (Acts 13:2, 4).

Nearly three decades ago, I received a call to enter full-time, vocational Gospel ministry. No person came to me and said I ought to be a preacher. The directive came from God, through the working of the Holy Spirit. Several years later, I experienced an ordination service at my first church. Several men, some whom I had known all my life, came and laid their hands on me. There was nothing magical or mysterious about this. It was simply the Holy Spirit's way of placing His stamp of approval on my call and commending me for service.

Are you experiencing restlessness in your soul as you read these words? Perhaps the Holy Spirit is nudging you toward a fresh assignment. Be open and obedient to His leading as extreme fulfillment is there to be received.

"BE FILLED WITH THE SPIRIT"

Observe also, the Spirit **fills.** Why must a person be filled when the Holy Spirit has already come into our life when saved? For at least two reasons:

Scripture commands it—As Scripture states, *"Do not get drunk with wine, for that is dissipation, but be filled with the Spirit"* (Ephesians 5:18). Paul wrote these words to believers, which means they already possessed the Holy Spirit. Yet the baptism of the Spirit is positional rather than conditional.

He becomes a resident at the point of conversion, but that shouldn't be our ultimate aspiration. It's certainly not His. He would like to rise from occupant to head of the household, but can't do so without our cooperation. God initiates the baptism of the Spirit though the process of conviction and revelation. However, we as believers initiate His filling through confession, obedience and desire.

Life demands it—When asked why He continually stressed the need to be filled with the Spirit, the famed evangelist D.L. Moody responded, "Because I leak."[4] Let's face it, life is tough. Living in enemy occupied territory on this fallen planet, we need all the help we can get. Our only hope of abundant living is a fullness of the Holy Spirit.

Galatians 5:16 states: *"Walk by the Spirit, and you will not carry out the desire of the flesh."* This verse is perfectly illustrated by an account of a Sunday school teacher who gave his children a two-part assignment. The children were instructed to write for a half hour on two subjects, the Holy Spirit and the devil. One boy wrote diligently for the entire hour on the Holy Spirit, adding this note on the bottom of his paper: "I had no time for the devil." Being filled up with the Spirit and His blueprint for our lives keeps Satan at bay, snuffing out what he'd like to do.

To conclude, note carefully that it's the role of the third member of the Trinity to **restrain**. A respected religious leader from a previous generation once said concerning the decadent state of our society, "If the Holy Spirit was suddenly taken out of the world, 95 percent of the world would go on as usual." That's a catchy sound bite, one that I bought into early in my ministry. However, I've since realized it's not accurate. A more precise statement is: "The only reason conditions aren't much worse in the world today is because of the restraining power of the Holy Spirit."

"THE MAN OF LAWLESSNESS"

Paul addresses this in a letter to the Thessalonian church. A key reason he wrote to this congregation was to counteract false prophets who proclaimed that the Lord's second coming had already occurred. The apostle assured them that this would not happen until, *"the apostasy comes first, and the man of lawlessness is revealed, the son of destruction"* (2 Thessalonians 2:3). "Apostasy" refers to the tribulation, which has not yet begun; and "the man of lawlessness" to the antichrist, who remains unidentified at this point.

Paul continues, *"And you know what restrains him now, so that in his time he will be revealed. For the mystery of lawlessness is already at work; only **he** who now restrains will do so until **he** is taken out of the way"* (2 Thessalonians 2:6,7, emphasis added).

Although some commentators disagree, "he" in verse seven is clearly the Holy Spirit. In a fallen world in which the majority of the people are lost, the Spirit maintains a presence in our schools, businesses, government, and families, harnessing an onslaught of evil that will one day overflow its banks and break the dam, leaving destruction and death in its wake.

Why would a loving God let this happen? Because He's setting the stage for His Son to come again, this time to defeat His opposing armies, set up His millennial kingdom and usher in a new heaven and new earth. In the meantime, the third member of the Trinity is busy convicting, teaching, counseling, calling, restraining.

At an astounding 55.232 carats, the famed Sancy diamond resides in the French Grand Jewel collection at the Louvre. Once the largest white diamond in the Western world, the stone possesses a history teeming with mystery, tragedy, and intrigue. In the 16th century, a courier of France's King Henry IV was killed by thieves while en route with the precious stone. When the body was later interred, the valuable gem was discovered in the stomach of the messenger, who chose to swallow it rather than let it get into the hands of robbers.[5]

If you're a believer, you have something inside, Someone in fact, infinitely more valuable than the Sancy diamond. If not, there's no better time than the present to make that happen.

7

CONSTANT CONTACT

"Pray without ceasing"
(1 Thessalonians 5:17).

෨෩

During the Apollo missions to the moon, the spaceships were off course more than 90% of the time. Yet, through continual communication with Mission Control they could make necessary connections. In our journey through life, we too, are off course most of the time.[1] By staying in constant contact with God we can correct our course, stay headed in the right direction, and succeed in our mission. Along with regularly reading the Bible, the best means of maintaining a continuous connection is through prayer.

Because you are reading this book, I know you're interested in growing as a believer. That means you absolutely must develop a consistent prayer life. Scripture says *"Jesus Himself would often slip away to the wilderness and pray"* (Luke 5:16). If Jesus, God in the flesh and Savior of the world, needed to pray, then how much more do you and I?

If possible, make prayer the first thing you do in the morning. King David writes, *"In the morning, O LORD, You will hear my voice; In the morning I will order my prayer to You and eagerly watch"* (Psalm 5:3). If you are not a morning person or your lifestyle simply isn't conducive to such a plan, then don't fret over it. *That* you pray is far more important than *when* you pray.

It's great if you can breakaway for consistent, long stretches of prayer. You can settle your soul and create a better environment for communication with God. Maintaining a journal or prayer guide, perhaps even with songs and scripture, helps tremendously. However, don't make that the extent of your praying, or beat yourself up if you can't arrange it.

John Erskin, a well-known author and educator from a previous generation, learned what he calls the most valuable lesson of his life at 14, one that relates beautifully to prayer. When asked by his piano teacher, "How many times a week do you practice, and how long do you practice each time?" John replied that he usually tried to practice once a day, generally for an hour or more. The teacher warned, "Don't do that. When you grow up, time won't come in long stretches. Practice in minutes, whenever you can find them - five or ten before school, after lunch, between chores. Spread your practice throughout the day, and music will become a part of your life."

Sprinkle your petitions throughout the day to the point it becomes as natural and habitual as breathing. Also, be open and available to spontaneous prayers, either in person, via text or over the phone. God will open such opportunities to those sensitive to His Spirit. So don't delay, lest you forget.

BUILD A RELATIONSHIP

As you mine more deeply into this critical area of prayer, view it as a delight rather than duty. Make building a relationship with God a priority over getting something from Him. Looking at the big picture, a change in our hearts will prove more valuable than a change in our circumstances. We should "ask, seek, and knock," yet not before becoming more connected with the One able to give.

For example, what is your impression of a friend, family member, or co-worker who greets you with a barrage of requests without even bothering to engage in some introductory conversation? If you're a grandparent, how do you feel if your grandchild barges into the house and says, "give me this, do that, take me there, and fix this"? You'd like to do all these things, but wouldn't you rather they climb up in your lap, give you a big hug, and tell you first how much they love and appreciate you?

Come to God first with **praise and adoration,** a practice which biblical prayers often modeled. *"Because Your lovingkindness is better than life,"* said David, *"My lips will praise You"* (Psalm 63:1). Following the completion of the wall around Jerusalem, the spiritual leaders proclaimed, *"Stand up and praise the LORD your God, who is from everlasting to everlasting. Blessed be your glorious name and may it be exalted above all blessing and praise"* (Nehemiah 9:5).

Jesus provides the best example in the opening line of what has become known as The Lord's Prayer: *"Our Father in heaven, hallowed be your name"* (Matthew 6:9). *Hallowed* is a New Testament expression used only in reference to the name of God. The Greek word for our word *hallow* is *hagiazo,* meaning "to revere or sanctify." [2]

This comes first because it helps shift our focus from ourselves to God. Of course, we have needs, otherwise why would we have come to Him in prayer? However, building a relationship with God, as opposed to sharing our requests to Him, should be our priority.

"Since its source is God Himself, praise centers on the excellencies, perfections and glories of His nature, His character and His role in human affairs. It is the most appropriate way to enter His presence." [3] As we probe deeper into the matter, note these two biblical truths regarding praise.

Singing enhances praise—There is no better way to heighten your praise than expressing it through singing. Adoration through song in prayer creates a pleasant aroma that floats through the portals of heaven into the nostrils of God, bringing Him great joy. As the Psalmist writes, *"Come before him with joyful singing"* (Psalm 100:2). It may seem awkward at first, yet singing clearly invigorates prayer. It certainly works for me, as I make a joyful noise through simple praise songs or the choruses of my favorite hymns.

Satan hates praise—Just like singing ambushed the enemy in the days of King Jehoshaphat (2 Chronicles 20), you can keep Satan from infiltrating your prayers through the weapon of song. To him, our praises are worse than that screeching sound that comes when someone drags their fingernails down a chalk board. Why? Because as you will recall, Lucifer once served as praise leader of heaven before his pride and rebellion prompted God to remove him from that privileged position. "Satan is allergic to praise. So where there is massive triumphant praise, Satan is paralyzed, bound, and banished."[4] So heed the charge of Martin Luther by singing a Psalm to chase the devil away.

As the Spirit leads, make the transition in your praying to **gratitude and thanksgiving**. This differs from praise in that we are expressing appreciation to God for what He has done rather than adoring Him for who He is.

The Bible contains numerous references to thanksgiving and gratitude. After the ark was brought to Jerusalem and subsequent offerings made, David said, *"Oh give thanks to the LORD, call upon His name; Make known His deeds among the peoples"* (1 Chronicles 16:8).

The Gospels provide ample evidence that Jesus modeled a life of thankfulness. Before feeding the four thousand with a few loaves of bread and small fish, He gave thanks to the Father (Mark 8:6,7). Jesus said after a time of teaching, *"I thank thee, O Father, Lord of heaven and earth, because thou hast hid these things from the wise and prudent, and hast revealed them unto babes"* (Matthew 11:25, KJV).

Paul expressed the importance of thanksgiving repeatedly, penning, *"Singing and making melody with your heart to the Lord, always giving thanks for all the things in the name of our Lord Jesus Christ to God, even the Father. Be anxious for nothing, but in everything by prayer and supplication with thanksgiving let your requests be made known to God"* (Ephesians 5:19,20; Philippians 4:6).

Take a piece of paper and write down everything you can think of for which you are thankful. Include matters of eternal significance – such as salvation and a future home in heaven; as well as simple pleasures like singing birds, good food, and an open parking place.

List trials, as well as victories, since they may prove to be more valuable in the long run. Keep this list handy, continuing to update it as God works in your life.

"IF WE CONFESS OUR SINS . . ."

Next comes the sometimes unpleasant but always necessary time of **acknowledgment and confession.** Just because we know Christ doesn't mean we stop sinning. We all sin every day. The difference is the Holy Spirit inside us nudging our spirits, convicting us of that sin. Since transgressions separate us from and mar our relationship with God, we must acknowledge these sins before Him through prayer. As the Word says, *"If we confess our sins, He is faithful and righteous to forgive us our sins and to cleanse us from all unrighteousness"* (1John 1:9).

Take a few moments to meditate on these critical points related to confession.

- **Confession must first be to God, since all sin is ultimately against Him.**

- **Confession is agreeing with God concerning the seriousness of our sin.**

- **Confession should be carried out swiftly and specifically.**

- **Confession must be followed up with repentance and renewal.**

- **Confession can be prompted by a prayer for God's illumination**.

In 1884, Grover Cleveland ran against James G. Blaine for U. S. President. During the campaign, Blaine supporters discovered that Cleveland, a bachelor at the time, fathered a child by Mrs. Maria Crofts Halpin, an attractive widow who had been on friendly terms with numerous politicians.

To capitalize on the situation, they tried to pin an immorality tag on Cleveland by distributing flyers showing an infant titled, "One more vote for Cleveland" and by having crowds chant, "Ma, ma, where's my pa? Gone to the White House, Ha, Ha, Ha!" The move backfired badly when Cleveland chose to tell the truth and admit to the scandal. His confession diffused the issue and he eventually won the race.[5]

Coming clean before God is never a bad idea. As the Bible says, *"He who conceals his transgressions will not prosper, But he who confesses and forsakes them will find compassion"* (Proverbs 28:13). Carefully include acknowledgement and confession before moving into the next key component, praying on behalf of **people and circumstances.**

The Scriptural term for such praying is intercession, which typically means intervening for others and situations. I'd like to simplify the topic by zeroing in on these two challenges.

Focus first on the matters of spirituality and eternity—Most of the praying that takes place in our churches centers on temporal, mostly health related issues. As someone once quipped, "We pray more to keep saints out of heaven than sinners out of hell."

While such intercession is important, a careful study of prayers in the Bible reveals their emphasis on spirituality and eternity. Paul provides these ideal examples: *"I pray that the eyes of your heart may be enlightened, so that you will know what is the hope of His calling . . . that He would grant you, according to the riches of His glory, to be strengthened with power through His Spirit in the inner man . . ."* (Ephesians 1:18, 3:16).

Make a list of lost people you know and pray regularly for them. Ask that the Holy Spirit would convict those who've strayed away from the truth, and comfort those facing affliction.

Formulate a plan of intercession—For example, I pray for local leaders on Monday, state leaders on Tuesday, and national leaders on Wednesday. In addition to interceding for your immediate family every day, devote other days of the week to extended family. Also, I pray through the 50 U.S. and 228 countries in the world every 31 days.

There are so many ways to run with this. I highly recommend going to the web site of Every Home for Christ at www.EHC.org, where you'll discover a plethora of resources to help develop a plan.

"FAR BE IT FROM ME . . ."

In the wake of their idolatry and disobedience, the Israelites asked their leader Samuel to pray for them. In response, he said, *". . . far be it from me that I should sin against the LORD by ceasing to pray for you"* (1 Samuel 12:23). With these words in mind, take advantage of every opportunity to pray for others. And while you're at it, make sure you include the fifth vital element—praying for yourself, biblically known as **petitioning.**

A great biblical example of petitioning appears buried in the midst of an Old Testament genealogical list. Jabez, the subject of Bruce Wilkerson's wildly popular book, *The Prayer of Jabez*, asked for God's blessings, prosperity, and protection. (1 Chronicles 4:10).

Jesus included petitions when communicating with His Father, voicing in the Model prayer, *"Give us this day our daily bread"* (Matthew 6:11). On the eve of the crucifixion, He prayed, *"Father, glorify Me together with yourself, with the glory which I had with You before the world was"*(John 17:5).

Jesus was the recipient of numerous petitions as well. A man covered with leprosy pleaded with Him: *"Lord, if You are willing, You can make me clean"* (Luke 5:12). Ten men suffering with the same condition cried out, *"Jesus, Master, have mercy on us!"* (Luke 17:13). A blind man in Jericho called out, *"Lord, I want to regain my sight"* (Luke 18:41). All the above received the healing for which they petitioned.

There's certainly nothing selfish or presumptuous about praying for yourself as long as you're willing to line up your will with God's will for your life. As the Bible says, *"Delight yourself in the LORD, and He will give you the desires of your heart"* (Psalm 37:4).

"SPEAK FOR YOUR SERVANT IS LISTENING"

Understanding that it is not a monologue *to* God, but rather a dialogue *with* Him, consider the sixth and final facet of prayer—**listening**. This is the most neglected, yet potentially most precious part of prayer. After all, what could be better than hearing from God?

Like young Samuel, when God has a message for us, we should respond with, *"Speak, for Your servant is listening"*(1 Samuel 3:10), Isaiah penned, *"He awakens Me morning by morning, He awakens My ear to listen as a disciple"* (Isaiah 50:4).

One Wednesday night my wife wasn't feeling well and said she probably wouldn't make it to choir practice. Yet later, as I was walking down the hall near the music room, I heard her singing. *That can't be her*, I thought, I wasn't expecting her to come. When I walked out in the parking lot, there sat her car. After three plus decades of being together, I easily recognize her voice. In the same way, the more time you spend with God, the easier it will be to recognize His voice.

Although you may not hear Him audibly, God still speaks. Jesus said, *"My sheep hear My voice, and I know them, and they follow Me"* (John 10:27). Listen carefully for His "words." And, with the Spirit's help, apply the following stipulations.

Make sure it's His voice you are hearing—You have a target on your back when you get serious about your prayer life. The believer's soul enemies on this fallen planet, the *world*, the *flesh*, and the *devil*, arise with "voices" of their own to distract and derail.

I can say from experience that such assaults typically begin in the mind—especially when you sit down to pray. That's why, with the help of the Spirit, we must heed the command of the apostle Paul, *"destroying speculations and every lofty thing raised up against the knowledge of God . . . taking every thought captive to the obedience of Christ"* (2 Corinthians 10:5). Implementing military language, Paul commands us to mentally take as prisoner and incarcerate any thoughts that stand in opposition to God and the message He desires to communicate.

Take it a step further by speaking directly against the soul enemies and carnal ideas though the command of faith—aka authoritative prayer. The authority of Jesus, which you possess by way of the His shed blood and the Spirit's indwelling in your life, provides grounds for such intercession. God will not reveal anything to His children that stands in opposition to His Word and His will.

Act upon the message you receive—Remember that Jesus' sheep not only *hear* Him, but *follow* Him as well. His half-brother James said, *"But prove yourselves doers of the word, and not merely hearers, who delude themselves"* (James 1:22). Providing his own illustration for this command, he talked about the man who saw himself in the mirror, then walked away and immediately forgot what he looked like (James 1:23,24).

Even in our worldly, secular society, it's still acceptable, even fashionable to hear God's message. Hollywood has even gotten in on the act. However, interest dwindles when it comes to following and living out what's been presented.

As Scripture commands, *"Guard your steps as you go to the house of God and draw near to listen rather than to offer the sacrifice of fools"* (Ecclesiastes 5:1). Make what is often the most neglected part of prayer your most rewarding and anticipated.

Early African converts to Christianity were rigorous and regular in their private prayer times. Each one reportedly had a particular place in the brush where they would plead before God. Eventually, the paths to these spots became clearly worn. Consequently, if one of the believers became negligent in their devotions, the others would soon notice. They would then lovingly remind the lax one, "Brother, the grass grows on your path."[6]

Keep your path to God well-worn. Maintain constant contact, discovering the necessity and joy of "praying without ceasing."

8

UPON THIS ROCK

"Not forsaking our own assembling together . . ."
(Hebrews 10:25).

෨෪

A pastor decided to visit a non-attending member of his church who had once come regularly. Since it was a very cold day, the preacher found the man sitting by a blazing fire when he entered the house. The pastor sat in a chair gazing at the burning logs, but said nothing.

Several minutes later, the visitor took fire tongs and removed a bright orange ember from the pile of glowing logs, placing it alone at one side of the hearth. The host watched quietly as the once fiery piece of wood dimmed into cold grayness. With not a word spoken since the initial greetings, the minister glanced at his watch and rose to leave. On his way out, he placed the cooling wood back in the middle of the fire. Immediately, it began to burn and glow like the wood around it.

Someone asked a man once why he didn't go to church. "Because, I've been," he replied. Unfortunately, more and more people share that sentiment, especially in America. People who used to attend two or three times a month now go one or two. Having served as a senior pastor for over 25 years, I'd say our best potential for reaching people comes from the *dechurched*—those who once attended, but haven't for an extended period.

I sympathize with these folks. Clinging to memories and outdated methods, church can be boring and irrelevant. People in the church can be cliquish, judgmental, and temperamental. If someone tells me they won't come because of so many hypocrites in the church, I say, "Oh, come on anyway, there's always room for one more" (not really, though I have been tempted).

As imperfect as it can be, the church remains God's plan for reaching people locally, regionally, nationally, and internationally with the Gospel. With that in mind, let's delve first into the **start of the church.**

The English word "church" comes from the Greek *ekklesia,* which refers to those who have been "called out." The first time it appears in the New Testament was when Jesus told Peter, *"Upon this rock I will build My church"* (Mathew 16:18). Many believe the Lord is referring to Himself here, since Peter refers to Him as such (1 Peter 2:8). Others claim He is addressing Peter's confession of faith (Matthew 16:16). While I see merit in both explanations, I believe that the Lord is alluding to Peter the person. This assertion is based on what Jesus said when He called Peter to be a disciple. *"'You are Simon the son of John; you shall be called Cephas'* (which is translated Peter)." Both *Cephas* and *Peter* mean "rock" in their respective languages (Aramaic, Greek).

Jesus' declaration came to fruition a few months later, 50 days following Christ's resurrection in fact, in Jerusalem on the Jewish day of Pentecost. Peter the "rock" preached one of the most powerful sermons in the history of the Church. The Holy Spirit came, the people fell under conviction, 3,000 were converted and the church was birthed.

The church was considered a sect within Judaism at first because most Christ's original followers were Jews. In fact, they maintained their loyalty to Mosaic Law and continued involvement at the temple or synagogue. Over time, often because of persecution, these Jewish Christian leaders understood that, because God so loved the world, they must take seriously Jesus' command to *"Go therefore and make disciples of all nations"* (Matthew 28:19).

THE CHURCH

That small but determined band of believers obeyed the Lord's command, spreading the Gospel beyond their borders. Let's now examine the **scope of the church,** how the church and its churches have multiplied into hundreds of millions of followers in the past 2,000 years.

The church in general—Means all believers in every age. The term "is used in the generic sense to refer to the overall fellowship of the redeemed without respect to locality or time."[1] It is what Jesus meant when He said, "Upon this rock I will build my church."

This makes no reference to a specific congregation or denomination. The most concentrated use of church in this manner appears in Paul's letter to the believers in Ephesus. *"And He (God) put all things in subjection under His (Christ's) feet, and gave Him (Christ) as head over all things to the church, which is His (Christ's) body, the fullness of Him (Christ) who fills in all"* (Ephesians 1:22,23; see also 3:10, 21; 5:23-32). God has placed everything under the power and authority of Christ, who is the head of the church. It's going to be a glorious celebration when believers of all ages will assemble in one place at the Lord's return. The significance of the church in general will be revealed then.

The local church—"The local church is the visible operation of the church."[2] This includes all congregations that have ever or ever will exist, including the one you may attend. Of the 115 times that *ekklesia* appears in the New Testament, 92 of them refer to the local church.[3] This leaves no doubt as to the importance of the local churches' role in first century kingdom expansion.

This brings to mind a phrase coined in recent years, "all politics are local." That quip can be applied to the "church" as well. Para church organizations and media ministries have their place and often serve as faith catalysts, yet nothing can take the place of the local church.

WE ARE CHRIST'S BODY

The Bible is full of imagery, especially when it comes to the church. These **symbols of the church** will provide a greater understanding of its role on this fallen earth.

Body—This is the most common symbol for the church used by Paul in his letters. It makes perfect sense, since the body is a very *common* thing. We all have one. They're everywhere. It's the same with the church. Even though its function is otherworldly in nature, it's a very earthly fellowship— made up of very ordinary people— that crosses cultural, racial, and economical barriers.

On the flipside, like the body, the church is very *complex*. Only God could fashion these temporal tabernacles in which we live, with their intricate combination of bones, muscle, organs, nerves, etc. Likewise, only God could unite a diverse, sin-prone, self-centered group of people behind a common purpose.

As the Bible says, *"For just as we have many members in one body and all the members do not have the same function, so we, who are many, are one body in Christ, and individually members of one another"* (Romans 12:4,5). Just as the human body is made up of a myriad of internal and external parts, all working together for one purpose, the church is made up of uniquely gifted people striving toward a common cause.

Unity doesn't mean uniformity. As the body of Christ, the church is much greater than the sum of its parts. *"Christ also is the head of the church, He Himself being the Savior of the body. Because we are all members of His body"* (Ephesians 5:23,30).

Vineyard —We move next from the body to the soil. Since biblical history plays out in an agricultural society, it makes perfect sense that a symbol of the church would emerge from this realm.

The clearest Biblical example comes by way of a parable told by Jesus (Matthew 21:33-46). In this story a man plants a vineyard, which signifies Christ planting the church. The vineyard farmers kill the owner's servants, and eventually his son, when they come to collect the fruit. These servants represent the Old Testament prophets who proclaimed the uncompromising message of God. Obviously, the son in the parable signifies Jesus, who dealt with the symbol of the vine in more detail in the Upper Room on the night before His crucifixion. There, He emphasized the vital connection between the church and its life-giving Source. He said, *"I am the vine; you are the branches. If a man remains in me and I in him, he will bear much fruit"* (John 15:5). Just like a hand is helpless without receiving orders from the brain, the branch will remain fruitless without proper connection to the vine.

Like a bunch of brown and dying limbs that have been trimmed from a nearby tree, so will be the fate of a church and its members that separate themselves from the One who loves them and gave Himself for them.

Flock—This is another agricultural image for the church used in the New Testament. Since Jesus is called the "Good Shepherd" (John 10:11), the "Great Shepherd" (Hebrews 13:20), and the "Chief Shepherd," it's only fitting that His followers, the church, would be characterized individually as sheep and corporately as a flock.

Sheep are vulnerable and defenseless. In biblical times, and still in many parts of the world, they rely on their shepherd for direction to food and protection against wild animals. They also depend on one another, as a lone sheep is especially susceptible to danger.

Jesus' words to His disciples, *"Fear not little flock"*(Luke 12:32), are just as pertinent today as they were 2,000 years ago. Since, like a hungry coyote, our *"adversary, the devil, prowls around like a roaring lion, seeking someone to devour"* (1 Peter 5:8), as a church and its members, we must depend on Christ for protection and provision rather than trying to survive on our own strength.

Family—When you were born, you became part of a physical family. If you're born again, you belong to a spiritual family, the church. You have or had a father, otherwise you wouldn't be here. As a believer, you have God as your Father. Your fellow believers are brothers and sisters in Christ. Scripture says, *"You are all sons of God through faith in Christ Jesus"* (Galatians 2:26). Therefore, church is not a place we *go* to, but a family we *belong* to. More importantly than traveling to a *place* this Sunday, you are connecting with *people*.

For much of our vocational ministry, my wife and I have been separated a rather long distance from our extended family. In recent years, our daughters have gone to college, later marrying and moving to start lives of their own. You can see why then, we need our church family now more than ever. You can also see why Paul refers to *"the church of the living God, the pillar and support of the truth,"* as a *"household of God"* (1 Timothy 3:15).

Building—Since a household needs a place to live, this verse dovetails nicely into the one above: *"You also, as living stones, are being built up as a spiritual house"* (1 Peter 2:5). I preach on Sundays at a church made of brick and mortar. More importantly, on those days I fellowship with other "living stones." While gathered in a visible, temporal structure, we worship together as an invisible, eternal building. And best of all, *"Having been built on the foundation of the apostles and prophets,* this "spiritual structure" has as its cornerstone *"Christ Jesus Himself"* (Ephesians 2:20).

Bride—No symbol speaks more prominently of Jesus' great love for the church than this one. And if the church is the bride, then obviously Christ is the bridegroom. John the Baptist made reference to this as Jesus was about to begin His public ministry: *"'I am not the Christ but am sent ahead of him.' The bride belongs to the bridegroom. The friend who attends the bridegroom waits and listens for him, and is full of joy when he hears the bridegroom's voice"* (John 3:28-29).

Paul picked up on this in one of his letters to the church at Corinth. He said, *"I am jealous of you with a godly jealousy. I promised you to one husband, to Christ, so that I might present you as a pure virgin to him"* (2 Corinthians 11:2). Unfortunately, the Corinthians had strayed from their pure devotion to Christ, which was part of what prompted Paul to write to them.

The most exciting part of this bride/bridegroom relationship is yet to come. At the end times, when Christ returns, the wedding between the Lamb (Christ) and His bride (the church) will be celebrated with a supper (Revelation 19:7, 9). Only born again believers whose names are written in the Lamb's Book of Life will attend this great feast (Matthew 22:1-14). Later, after Satan's final defeat and the judgment of the lost, the Holy City, the New Jerusalem (the church), will come down from heaven to the new earth as a bride beautifully dressed for her husband (Revelation 21:2).

Obviously, this list of symbols is not exhaustive. I do hope it gives you a clearer picture of who the church is and what she does. This last section, **the significance of the church,** provides further insight. Five key functions of the church came to mind as I considered this critical issue.

Accountability—This function of the church isn't a popular one, especially in this day of tolerance. "Don't judge me" is the cry of this generation, even in the church. And while it's certainly God's job to do the judging, it's ours to keep a watchful eye out for our friends and family in Christ.

Some may say otherwise, but most people want to be noticed and welcome contact when they fall away from the fellowship. We are our brother's keeper. The Bible says, *"Iron sharpens iron, So one man sharpens another"* (Proverbs 27:17). Never underestimate the potential you have to influence others, and vice versa. *"Encourage one another day after day, as long as it is called 'Today,' so that none of you will be hardened by the deceitfulness of sin"*(Hebrews 3:13).

Community—Concerning the early church, *"They were continually devoting themselves to the apostles' teaching and to **fellowship**, to the breaking of bread and to prayer"* (Acts 2:42, emphasis added). The word in the original language for fellowship is *koinonia*. It means "sharing in common, communion" and is used 20 times in the New Testament. We desperately need this fellowship, perhaps more than ever, in this high–tech, low–touch world saturated with too much information and too little interaction. And the church is the premier place to find this *koinonia*.

Instruction—Note from above that, in addition to fellowship, the Jerusalem believers devoted themselves to the apostles' teaching. Later in Acts, we encounter the congregation at Berea, who *"Were more noble-minded than those in Thessalonica, for they received the word with great eagerness, examining the Scriptures daily to see whether these things were so."* (Acts 17:11). In a world becoming increasingly biblically illiterate, we must follow the example of these early congregations. Our churches, along with help in the home, must be the standard bearer for solid instruction in Scriptural truth.

Missions—Soaking up all this fellowship and instruction *within* the church is fine, as long we squeeze out the sponge in ministry *beyond* our walls. We need to spend less time gazing in front of mirrors and more time peering out of windows. By the grace of God, with the help of the Spirit, I want to be an Acts 1:8 Christian. In this verse, Jesus challenged, *"You shall be My witnesses both in Jerusalem, and in all Judea and Samaria, and even to the remotest part of the earth."*

This isn't an "either/or," but rather a "both/and" when it comes to meeting physical and spiritual needs. It's also "both/and" when it comes to local and distant missions. Successful churches are visible in their communities—feeding the hungry, encouraging first-responders, assisting the schools, doing neighborhood cleanup, and of course, sharing the Gospel.

At the same time, opportunities for regional and overseas projects should be explored and made available. And if your church can serve by helping start a new congregation—whether through a plant, mission, or additional campus, that makes it all the better.

Worship—One word of warning, don't get so caught up in the work that you forget the One behind it all. All of the above are vitally important, yet we must always remember that God is to be the object of our devotion. Sometimes we get so stoked by *doing,* that we neglect the importance of *being.* Gathering on a regular basis with God's people for corporate worship helps us keep that proper perspective.

David, who said, *"Zeal for your house consumes me,"* also wrote, *"I rejoiced with those who said to me, 'Let us go to the house of the Lord'"* (Psalm 69:9, 122:1). The King, "a man after God's own heart" (1 Samuel 13:14), loved the LORD deeply and enjoyed nothing more than assembling with His people in humble praise and adoration.

> All his life, Old Bill had never gone to church; no matter how much he was coaxed, he could never be persuaded to attend even on Christmas and Easter. "When it *freezes in June*," he would say, "then I will go to church." One year it was unusually cold and stayed that way until late spring. The first part of June the mercury dipped to freezing for several nights. Everyone thought about Old Bill and what he had said. Perhaps this spell of cold weather would force him to attend church. It did! One Sunday Old Bill made his first appearance in the meeting house—while the organ played softly—*six men carried him in*!

If you're a part of a local church family, attend as often as you can and serve in any way you can. If not, don't be like Old Bill and wait till you can't enjoy the experience.[4]

Todd Gaddis

9

THROW OUT THE LIFELINE

"How could I, unless someone guides me?"

(Act 8:31)

೫⌾೮

Imagine you're with friends aboard a pontoon boat on the lake when all of a sudden you hear screaming and see splashing from someone drowning just a few yards away, moments away from death. Assessing the situation, you spot a life preserver connected to a rope attached to the back of the boat. Calmly and quickly, you detach the ring and toss it beside the distressed swimmer. Before long, that person is safely aboard your craft headed for land.

People all around you are drowning in sin, tragically headed for the second death, which is infinitely worse than physical drowning. As a born again believer, you have in your possession a Lifeline, Someone who can save them and provide their escape from eternal separation from God. Are you willing to take a few minutes of your time and point them to Jesus?

The best thing that could ever happen to you on this fallen earth is discovering Christ as Savior. The second best thing is leading someone else to faith in Him. Sadly, statistics indicates most believers never experience this privilege that far exceeds anything this world has to offer.

Let's examine someone who specialized in throwing out spiritual lifelines. His name is Philip and he was among the original seven deacons in the early church. As we delve into a scene from this life, recorded in Acts 8:26-37, note first that God **prompts those sensitive to His purpose.**

Philip was preaching in the villages of Samaria when an angel sent him south to Gaza. While on his way, he ran across a high-ranking government official returning to Ethiopia from Jerusalem. At that point, *"The Spirit said to Philip, 'Go up and join this chariot'"* (Acts 8:29).

Later in the book of Acts, as Paul and Silas traveled on one of their missionary journeys, the Holy Spirit stopped them from a planned speaking stop. Then, a man appeared to Paul in a vision, pleading, *"Come over to Macedonia and help us"* (Acts 16:9). They answered the appeal, a move which opened doors for the spread of the Gospel into Europe.

I can't tell you the number of times the Holy Spirit has nudged my heart or arranged for a divine appointment in which I needed to share a word with someone about Christ. I haven't always obeyed the call yet never regretted when I did.

I heard a layman speak at a conference several years ago who had led hundreds of people to faith in Christ. When asked the secret to his success he answered, "I prayed for a burden."

As you consider this life changing subject of witnessing and evangelism, be open to the arrangements God will make for you to present your story. If you haven't heard from Him, pray for a burden for lost people, asking Him to make that happen for you. You'll soon realize that He **prepares those who haven't discovered the truth.**

Our text tells us that not only had the traveler gone to Jerusalem to worship, he was reading from the prophet Isaiah when Philip came along. Likely, this identifies him as a "God-fearer," a Gentile follower of God. Peter later encounters another such person named Cornelius, a devout military man whom God had primed and prepped to receive the Gospel (Acts 10:1-8).

Twenty centuries later, our communities, and churches too, teem with people just like the two men just mentioned. Though not yet converted, they certainly show curiosity and interest. Like that wee little man Zaccheus, they've made a spiritual climb up a sycamore tree to catch a better glimpse of Jesus.

THE SPIRIT CONVICTS

A key principle I remember from my evangelistic training is that the Holy Spirit works in the lives of all unbelievers. He convicts lost people of their sin and attests to the truth of God's Word being presented.

So, it should bring you great comfort to know that God plows the ground and prepares a seedbed before you ever come along. Of course, that's no guarantee the person will respond positively. We've all been given a free will. There's always the possibility that the person to whom you are ministering will resist the work of the Spirit. Fortunately, the official was receptive and ready for the evangelist's message. And as Philip discovered, God not only prompts those sensitive to His purpose, He **provides for those willing to obey.**

Most Christians won't share their faith because they don't know what to say or fear saying the wrong thing. Don't let the enemy discourage from sharing the gift of eternal life with others. Creator God, Christ in you, will not only provide the words, He will interpret what the person hears.

Jesus told His disciples they would be brought before various officials, *"But when they hand you over, do not worry about how or what you are to say; for it will be given you in that hour what you are to say. For it is* not you who speak, but it is the Spirit of your Father who speaks in you" (Matthew 10:19,20).

As you contemplate and consider the need to throw out the lifeline to those lost, first consider **asking questions.** *"Do you understand what you are reading?"* were the first words out of Philip's mouth as he approached the chariot.

Studying the earthly ministry of Jesus, you'll discover that asking questions was a primary part of His teaching method. In his book *All That Jesus Asks,* Stan Guthrie covers nearly 300 questions the Lord asked during His public ministry.[1] No doubt hundreds more were asked that didn't make it into the Gospels.

Questions serve as good conversation starters because they give the person a chance to talk about themselves and tell their story. Possibilities for openers include: Where are you in your spiritual journey? Have you given thought to life after death? Do you have the assurance you'll go to heaven when you die? Do you have a personal relationship with Jesus?

Philip started with Scripture since that's what the Ethiopian was reading at the time. In response to the evangelist's question, the official had one of his own, asking, *"How could I (understand), unless someone guides me?"* (Acts 8:31).

This is why you not only must be willing to ask questions, but *offer explanations* as well. What if Philip had said: "I'd like to help, but I'm really not sure what to say. Let me go find someone who knows the answers." This divine moment would have been spoiled and the Ethiopian might have ended up in hell. Fortunately, following a second question from the official, Philip began with the Scripture the official was reading and, *"preached Jesus to him"* (Acts 8:35).

"ALWAYS BEING READY"

I can't tell you the number of times I've had people bring friends and family to me, particularly children, for me to lead them through the salvation process. I'm always thrilled to help, yet part of me wishes they had done so themselves. You can do it, especially since you have something available to you Philip didn't–the New Testament. As the Word says, *"Sanctify Christ as Lord in your hearts, always being ready to make a defense to everyone who asks you to give an account for the hope that is in you"* (1 Peter 3:15). This four-part plan of salvation presentation should help.

God's desire—According to the Bible, *"God our Savior. . . desires all men to be saved and to come to the knowledge of the truth . . .not wishing for any to perish but for all to come to repentance"* (1 Timothy 2:4, 2 Peter 3:9). Does that mean everyone will be saved? Sadly, no. *"For the gate is small and the way is narrow that leads to life, and there are few who find it"* (Matthew 7:14).

God knows everyone who is and eventually will be saved. But we don't, which is why we must be diligent in fulfilling His desire to reach as many as possible.

Our problem—Scripture records, *"For all have sinned and fall short of the glory of God. For the wages of sin is death"* (Romans 6:23). This doesn't mean we become sinners the first time we do something bad. With the blood of Adam flowing through our veins, we are born into sin. As David acknowledged, *"Surely I was sinful at birth, sinful from the time my mother conceived me"* (Psalm 51:5, NIV).

For centuries, people have tried to earn their way out of this sin problem. All the good deeds and noble works we can muster can't begin to wipe away our transgressions and iniquities. As the Word proclaims, *"All of our righteous deeds are like a filthy garment"* (Isaiah 64:6). Fallen man's only hope is:

God's love—The Bible says, *"For God so **loved** the world, that He gave His only begotten Son,"* as well as, *"God demonstrates His own **love*** *toward us, in that while we were yet sinners, Christ died for us"* (Romans 5:8, emphasis added). The word in the original language in both cases comes from *agape,* which is unconditional, sacrificial, and selfless love. Even when we are most unlovable, God still loves us. There's nothing we can do to make Him stop loving us.

> A certain medieval monk announced he would be preaching next Sunday evening on "The Love of God." As the shadows fell and the light ceased to come in through the cathedral windows, the congregation gathered. In the darkness of the altar, the monk lighted a candle and carried it to the crucifix. First, he illumined the crown of thorns, next, the two wounded hands, then the marks of the spear wound. In the hush that fell, he blew out the candle and left the chancel. There was nothing else to say.[2]

Our requirement—Christ's death, burial, and resurrection does not automatically secure salvation. A response is required on our part. *"If you confess with your mouth Jesus as Lord, and believe in your heart God raised Him from the dead, you will be saved"* (Romans 10:9).

Confessing Jesus as Lord carries with it a two-pronged requirement. First it must be done with the mouth, which is an outward confirmation. Spoken words provide audible evidence of commitment to Christ. Inward, invisible affirmation takes place in the heart. Head knowledge is a good start but completed salvation requires a circumcision of the heart through the work of the Holy Spirit (Romans 2:29).

SET THE HOOK

At some point in the conversation you'll need to transition from offering explanations to **seeking a decision.** In the business world, it's called "asking for the order" or "closing the deal." To a fisherman, it's "setting the hook" or "drawing in the net."

And once again, you'll find at this stage, questi(
Ask them if they understand what you've been (
clarification, review the following steps concerning wh
to be saved.

1. Admit your need (I am a sinner).

2. Be willing to turn from your sins (repent).

3. Believe that Jesus Christ died for you on the cross and rose from the grave.

If they agree with the above, ask them if they are willing to pray to receive Christ. They can do so in their own words or use the following "sinner's prayer" as a guide.

Dear God, I know that Jesus is Your Son, and that He died on the cross and was raised from the dead. I know I have sinned and need forgiveness. I am willing to turn from my sins and receive Jesus as my Savior and Lord. Thank You for saving me. In Jesus' name, Amen.

Since they usually choose the latter, go through a few words of the prayer at a time and have them repeat after you. This may seem canned to some, but if they mean what they say, it's acceptable. Countless couples have said vows to get married, so we can certainly repeat prayers to get saved.

And once that has happened and you wrap up the prayer with a few words of your own, begin by welcoming this brand-new Christian into the family of God. Reassure them that God heard the prayer, the angels are rejoicing, and their names have been recorded in heaven. Warn that the enemy will try to get them to doubt this decision, confirming again this is a commitment based on faith, not feelings. As Paul writes, *"For by grace you have been saved through faith; and that not of yourselves, it is the gift of God"* (Ephesians 2:8).

Conclude by stressing the importance of regular prayer and Bible reading/study. Help them get plugged into a small group and corporate worship at a church if they haven't done so already. Mentoring them yourself through the discipleship process would be even better. And ask them to take what they just heard and share it with a lost person they know. New Christians, with fresh testimonies, make great "fishers of men."

When Charles Wesley experienced the joy of divine forgiveness, he told a Moravian friend of his new sense of pardon, and added, "I suppose I had better keep silent about it."

"Oh, no, my brother," came the reply. "If you had a thousand tongues, you should go and use them all for Jesus." Charles Wesley went home and wrote the following hymn:

> "O for a thousand tongues to sing
> My great Redeemer's praise,
> The glories of my God and King,
> The triumphs of his grace!"

If you know Christ as your Savior, don't keep silent about it. Don't be ashamed of the gospel, *"for it is the power of God for salvation to everyone who believes"* (Romans 1:16). Request and receive a burden for the spiritually drowning—then "throw out the lifeline."

10

"LOOK! WATER!"

"What prevents me from being baptized?"
(Acts 8:36).

∽◌◌

In case you're wondering, at the end of his discussion with Philip, the Ethiopian spotted water and wanted to be baptized. Philip answered, *"If you believe with all your heart, you may."* The official answered and said, *"I believe that Jesus Christ is the Son of God"* (Acts 8:37). Philip then ordered the chariot to stop, after which they went to the water where he baptized him.

This encounter supports the first of eight principles I'd like to address in this chapter: **Baptism follows salvation.** We see this confirmed when Philip ministered in Samaria. *"But when they believed Philip preaching the good news about the kingdom of God and the name of Jesus Christ, they were being baptized, men and women alike"* (Acts 8:12). This is a key issue in the area of baptism, especially as it relates to the following:

Infant baptism—Although there is no biblical precedent for it, some Christian denominations baptize babies. This does not qualify as scriptural baptism because infants have not reached an age of

77

accountability, and therefore have no awareness of sin and God's plan of salvation.

Jewish babies, including Jesus, were circumcised according to the law at eight days of age (Leviticus 12:3, Luke 2:27). Hannah dedicated Samuel to the LORD at the Temple after she had weaned him. However, water was not a part of either occasion.

We dedicate babies at our church, as do most evangelical congregations. It is one of the most beautiful and meaningful events that takes place throughout the year, especially for the participating families. Even if water is part of the ceremony, I see nothing wrong with that, if it is viewed as a dedication service and not the true believer's baptism.

Adult conversion—Countless believers made decisions, walked the aisle, joined the church, and got baptized as children, yet didn't experience true conversion until years later, often as adults. This issue is especially near and dear to my heart because I am one of these. I was a lost church member for 14 years and a non-baptized believer for six years after that. I was a husband, father, and seminary graduate before properly settling this.

Like salvation, baptism is a one-time event. Although some people feel the need to repeat the process after a rededication or renewed commitment, it's not necessary. However, one needs to "get the order right" and get baptized if they've never done so or be if they experience true conversion later in life.

Understand next, that **baptism is an act of obedience**. Some denominations teach that going into the water actually saves a person, but like infant baptism, this too is biblically incorrect. Salvation comes, not by works, but as a gift. Nothing we do, including baptism, can save us. Only the shed blood of Christ can wash away our sins (1 John 1:7). The repentant thief on the cross was never baptized, yet he joined Jesus in paradise immediately upon his death.

Don't, however, take baptism lightly. I wouldn't have devoted a full chapter to the subject were it not extremely important. It isn't an option for the believer, but rather a command. As Peter preached to the crowd at Pentecost, *"Repent, and each of you be baptized in the name of Jesus Christ for the forgiveness of your sins"* (Acts 2:38).

I've said to scores of children in baptism counseling over the years, "If your parents ask you to do something and you don't, you've disobeyed, but have not ceased to be their child." Likewise, if God asks you to be baptized and you fail to do it, although you've disobeyed, you still belong to Him.

Comprehend also that ***baptism is a symbol.*** The Bible is full of symbols. A rainbow symbolizes God's covenant, trumpets—His speaking, a lamb—Christ's sacrifice, a dove—the Holy Spirit, and dry bones—spiritual death. Baptism depicts the cleansing provided by the death, burial and resurrection of Jesus Christ.

The gold band I've worn on the ring finger of my left hand for 33 years doesn't make me married. The vows I made before God and witnesses in the wedding ceremony sealed the covenant. Baptism doesn't save me, yet outwardly represents the change that has taken place inwardly.

A PICTURE OF SALVATION

During baptism counseling sessions, I'll often show the candidate a photo of my wife and ask them to identify her. When they say, "That's Mrs. Gaddis" and I respond, "No, that's not her," they look at me in disbelief. After a long pause, I'll say, "That's a *picture* of my wife, she's upstairs in her Sunday school class." Baptism is not salvation, but a picture of what has taken place.

Also, notice that ***baptism identifies one with Jesus.*** As Scripture says, *"We have been buried with Him through baptism into death,* *so that as Christ was raised from the dead through the glory of the Father, so we too might walk in the newness of life"* (Romans 6:4).

R.G. Lee was visiting Gordon's Calvary at Jerusalem, possibly the site where Jesus was crucified. Lee told the Arab guide he wanted to walk to the top of the hill. At first the guide tried to discourage him, but when he saw that Lee was determined to go, he went along. Once on the crest, Lee removed his hat and stood with bowed head, greatly moved. "Sir," asked the guide, "have you been here before?"

"Yes," replied Lee, "2,000 years ago."

All born again believers were there. "How can that be?" you ask. Our sins were nailed to the cross along with Jesus. *I have been crucified with Christ. For if we have become united with Him in the likeness of His death, certainly we shall also be in the likeness of His resurrection"* (Galatians 2:20, Romans 6:5).

Spiritually speaking, baptism illustrates the Gospel. Our submergence in water takes us back to the time of His death. Our coming out of the water points ahead to the time when, just as He was resurrected, we shall be as well.

Observe too that **baptism is pleasing to God.** I've baptized scores of new believers over the past three decades and I've never seen one unhappy about it. Most emerge from the water smiling, realizing their sins have been forgiven and their names have been recorded in heaven. The congregation often applauds with approval. A band of extended family beams with pride and gratitude. Mom and Dad shed tears and snap pictures. Yet no one is more thrilled than God Himself.

"I AM WELL PLEASED"

Before Jesus launched into public ministry, His cousin John baptized Him in the Jordan River. As the Holy Spirit descended in the form of a dove, God said, *"This is My beloved Son, in whom I am well pleased"* (Matthew 3:17). The Father's favor rested upon Jesus because His obedient, humble, self-emptying Son was about to fulfill a plan of redemption set in motion before the foundation of the world.

Obviously, Christ wasn't baptized to depict forgiveness of sin. So why did He do it? In addition to forming a connection with the "forerunner" John the Baptist, He provided an example, affirmed His humanity and played a part in displaying the unification of the Triune God.

Note next that **baptism is by immersion.** The word *baptize*, which means "to immerse," is taken directly from the Greek. At that time, in the marketplace, it was a word used when cloth was submerged in dye to make it a different color, or vegetables being immersed in vinegar to produce pickles.

I've seen the 15th Century Piero painting in which John the Baptist pours a bowl of water over the head of Jesus. Yet the Bible says, *"coming up out of the water, He (Jesus) saw the heavens opening"* (Mark 1:10). Later, *"John also was baptizing in Aenon near Salim, because there was much water there"* (John 3:23).

I still view this as a matter of interpretation. I believe the Bible teaches immersion but it's not a Gospel game-changer. I sprinkled a lady in a nursing home once who could not be immersed because of physical limitations. There will be believers in Heaven who have been sprinkled, as well as those not baptized at all.

Understand also that **baptism is an ordinance of the church.** "An ordinance is a **command** to be obeyed. It works no grace or special spiritual operation. The two ordinances of the church (baptism and Lord's Supper) are **visible** enactments of the Gospel message that Christ lived, died, was raised from the dead, ascended to heaven, and will someday return. Put simply, the church ordinances are visual **aids** to help us better understand and appreciate what Jesus Christ accomplished for us in His redemptive work."[1]

To be characterized as a New Testament church ordinance, a practice must be **instituted** by Christ (Matthew 28:19-20), **taught** by the apostles (Romans 6:3-4, Acts 19:1-5), and **practiced** by the early church (Acts 2:41; Acts 8:26-40). "Baptism and the Lord's Supper are (the) only rites for which such marks can be claimed, there can *only* be two ordinances."[2]

Typically, when I immerse someone, they are being baptized into the membership of our local church. There have been rare occasions over the years when I have baptized friends, family, or mission field candidates who weren't joining a church. Some won't join our church because we require immersion and they feel the sprinkling they received suffices. I simply leave that between them and the Lord and don't worry about it.

A SERMON WITHOUT WORDS

Finally see that **baptism is a way of confessing Christ.** I've told candidates often through the years that they're going to preach a better sermon than me without having to say a word. The fact that they have the courage to become the focal point of the service, stand in the baptistery before the congregation, and undergo immersion silently, but boldly states they have undergone a spiritual change and are taking a stand for Jesus.

This may seem normal for someone raised in a Christian environment, but for a person coming from a different faith, it's often unsettling. For instance, Hindus and Muslims who become believers are often ostracized, sometimes beaten and forced to move away from family and friends. You can pray to receive Christ privately and quietly, yet baptism is an overt declaration which draws a line in the sand.

Yet, any persecution from people is far overshadowed by the benefits of knowing God. As Jesus said, *"Everyone who confesses Me before men, the Son of Man will confess him also before the angels of God"* (Luke 12:8). As we stand before men on earth, bearing witness to our faith, Jesus proclaims before the angels in heaven that He died for us and we belong to Him.

Aengus, Christian king of Ireland, was baptized by St. Patrick in the middle of the fifth century. During the rite, St. Patrick inadvertently leaned on his sharp-pointed staff and stabbed the king's foot. Later, after looking down at the blood, realizing what he had done, and begging for forgiveness, the Saint asked the king, "Why did you suffer this pain in silence?" "I thought it was part of the ritual," the king replied.[3]

Although baptism should never be viewed as a ritual, it certainly signifies a connection to blood, the precious blood of Christ shed for the cleansing of our sins.

Todd Gaddis

11

MISCONCEPTIONS ABOUT GIVING

"God loves a cheerful giver"
(2 Corinthians 9:7).

ॐ

A sixty-two-year-old man, suffering from a rare disease that makes a person want to eat money, recently walked into the emergency room of the Cholet General Hospital in western France. "French doctors were taken aback when they discovered the reason for the patient's sore and swollen belly: He had swallowed around 350 coins: $650 worth."

The man had a history of psychiatric illness and his family warned physicians that he sometimes swallowed coins. A few had been taken from his stomach in past hospital visits.

Nevertheless, doctors gazed amazed at what they saw on the x-ray. An enormous opaque mass, found to weigh twelve pounds, showed up in the patient's stomach. It was so heavy that it forced the man's stomach down between his hips. Five days after the man's arrival, doctors removed his stomach and its contents. Sadly, the pitiful patient died with days. [1]

I can think of many safer and more responsible things to do with money besides eating it; such as spending it, saving it, and giving it away. Eighteenth century theologian and Methodist founder John Wesley once preached a sermon on the use of riches. His first point was "Earn all you can." An old miser sitting in the congregation nudged his neighbor and whispered, "I never heard preaching the like of that before. Yon man has good things in him." Then Wesley went on to denounce thriftlessness and waste and said, "Save all you can." The lover of money rubbed his hands together in glee and thought that with all the wealth he had piled up, he was certainly on the right track. But then Wesley made his last point with emphasis, "*Give all you can!*" The old miser was beside himself with despair, "Aw dear, aw dear," he exclaimed aloud, "now he's gone and spoiled it all!" [1]

Unfortunately, such feelings concerning money prevail today, even in our Christian circles. Thankfully, the Bible says a great deal about the subject. A key example appears in one of Paul's letters to the church at Corinth. After reading the text in 2 Corinthians 8:1-7, note carefully the following four misconceptions about giving.

First, **you've got to have extra money to be a giver.** I've heard people say, "I just wish I earned more money, so I'd have some to give away." The truth is, if you don't give when you have a little, you probably won't if you get a lot.

"BEYOND THEIR ABILITY"

Churches and other religious entities throughout the world receive their primary support from ordinary people, many living paycheck to paycheck. That was certainly the case with the Macedonian churches Paul writes about, who despite their poverty and affliction, gave *"beyond their ability"* (2 Corinthians 8:3).

Jesus, who often spoke about this issue, sat in the temple watching rich people put large amounts of money into the treasury, when a poor widow walked up and gave two small coins worth a cent. Seizing a teaching moment, the Lord said to His disciples, *"Truly I say to you, this poor widow put in more than all the contributors to the treasury; for they all put in out of their surplus, but she, out of her poverty, put in all she owned, all she had to live on"* (Luke 21:3,4).

Mr. Bill, an elderly black man, faithfully attended the first church I served in western Kentucky. He especially loved singing in the choir and attending church softball games. I can remember visiting him at his old trailer situated on a cattle farm on the edge of town. The word was he had never married. He spent his life working on the farm during the day and serving the owner's meals at night.

A few years after I moved from there, Mr. Bill went on to be with the Lord. In addition to a legacy of service, faithfulness and humility, he left behind nearly $100,000 to his church that desperately needed it after a fire destroyed their building. He was the last person one would expect to leave a gift of such magnitude, a man who couldn't even read or write.

I have a friend in the community named Johnny who, after spending three months in jail in 2001, was radically saved. I know it wasn't a whim because he remains intensely committed to this day. When his church recently ran a campaign to support missionaries worldwide, he and his wife pledged over $200.00 weekly for a year, in addition to regular tithes and offerings. You might think they are wealthy but that's not the case. He makes a modest living running a small appliance repair business. He said that some weeks he doesn't earn enough to cover the pledge, but honors it anyway, adding, "You can't out-give God no matter how hard you try."

When drought struck Israel in the days of Elijah, God sent him to a poor widow for food. Despite having, *"only a handful of flour . . .and a little oil"* (1 Kings 17:12), she agreed to feed the hungry prophet. Miraculously, her oil and flour supply did not run out until the rain returned. Little becomes much when God takes control. Thinking you have to have a lot to be a generous giver is a myth.

A second misconception concerning giving is that **you have to twist arms in order to get people to participate.** This reminds me of the story of a wealthy, but stingy man who decided to give his daughter and future son-in-law $10,000 for their wedding present. Being one who didn't like emotional confrontations, he decided to send it through his assistant. When the man returned, the father asked, "Did they cry or anything when you gave the money?"

"Maybe for a minute or two" answered the assistant.

"A minute or two!" the father exclaimed. "I wailed for over an hour after writing the check."

That may be the way many approach contributing to kingdom causes, but it certainly wasn't the attitude of the Macedonian churches. According to Paul, they gave with an **"abundance of joy,"** (2 Cor. 8:2).

One of my favorite Christmas movies is *The Christmas Carol,* based on the Charles Dickens novel of the same name. I especially love the scene at the end where Scrooge, a changed man, wakes up on Christmas morning, looks out on a snowy London and gleefully throws money to a young lad to buy a prize turkey for Bob Cratchet's holiday meal.

According to the Bible, *"God loves a cheerful giver"* (2 Corinthians 9:7). The word for cheerful in the original language, used only here in the New Testament, is a form of *hilaros*. From *hilaros,* we get the English word hilarious. Attitude trumps amount every time. An open hand is even better when accompanied by a merry heart and smiling face.

"THEY BEGGED TO GIVE"

Note also that the Macedonians denounced the arm twisting myth by *pleading for the opportunity to give.* In fact, they begged, *"With much urging for the favor of participation in the support of the saints"* (2 Corinthians 8:4).

They asked, even pleaded for the opportunity to contribute to the work of the ministry. In this era of pledge cards, fundraisers, capital campaigns, televangelists, etc, it's hard to even fathom someone on the giving side of the equation pleading for the chance to contribute. And yet, that's exactly what happens when the love of God breaks through and fills the hearts of His people.

After the Israelites escaped the Egyptians, made their way into the wilderness and received the law, God commanded Moses to build the tabernacle. The people gave so much toward the construction project that Moses sent word throughout the camp to quit making and bringing materials because they had more than enough already. Can you imagine telling people in early October to stop tithing because the yearly budget had already been met?

Of course this doesn't mean that we stop making people aware of the needs. Moses got the ball rolling by informing them of God's plan and seeking their offerings. The point is, it's not manipulation, coercion, but God's Spirit that ignites true generosity. When Spirit-filled people see God at work, they'll willingly give.

Observe too, the misconception that **your giving should be sporadic, whenever you feel the urge.** The truth is, we should give on a regular, consistent basis. As Paul wrote to the Corinthians, *"On the first day of every week each one of you is to put aside and save, as he may prosper, so that no collections be made when I come"* (1 Corinthians 16:1).

Christians should give at least a tithe (ten percent of their income) to the church. The reason most people don't tithe is because they take care of all their obligations first, having little or nothing left over to give. I make a mortgage, credit card, phone, insurance, satellite television, dry cleaners, hardware, trash pickup, and electric bill payment monthly. In fact, some of them are automatically withdrawn from my checking account. Why would I not make absolutely sure I give back to God a portion of what He's given to me?

As pastor, I notice that members are always on the go, here one week gone the next. People get ill and sometimes just have to crash. I understand. I need and like to take a Sunday off now and then myself. We are still responsible for making sure our gift makes it to church, even if we don't. Of course, we can bring it the next time we come, but that can mound up in a hurry.

Lots of people prefer that their dollars go toward special projects and designated causes like the organ fund, stained glass windows, benevolence, etc. These and other causes are wonderful, but should never take the place of regular budget giving. If everyone gave as God directs, we would not have to make special appeals and hold capital campaigns.

I realize that many people are on fixed incomes and others get compensated on an irregular basis. God understands that. I'm not trying to be legalistic about the matter. I do, however, have a passion about church stewardship. It's not right that ten to twenty percent of the givers account for eighty percent or more of the giving. And it's certainly wrong when small disagreements lead a member to stop giving to the church.

Consider these words from America's first billionaire, the late John D. Rockefeller, who gave away more than $500 million, $5 billion in today's money. The founder of Standard Oil Company faithfully tithed his whole life, a practice he started as a child. Rockefeller recalled:

> I had to begin work as a small boy to help support my mother. My first wages amounted to $1.50 per week. The first week after I went to work, I took the $1.50

home to my mother and she held the money in her lap and explained to me that she would be happy if I would give a tenth of it to the Lord. I did, and from that week until this day I have tithed every dollar God has entrusted to me. And I want to say, if I had not tithed the first dollar I made I would not have tithed the first million dollars I made.

I've heard people say they can't afford to tithe. I say you can't afford *not* to. In fact, you're missing tremendous blessings if you don't. As the Bible says, *"'Bring the whole tithe into the storehouse, so that there may be food in My house, and test Me now in this,' says the LORD of hosts, 'if I will not open for you the windows of heaven and pour out for you a blessing until it overflows'"* (Malachi 3:10).

The final misconception about giving is that **it's all about the money**. Obviously, the Macedonian churches got it, since *"They first gave themselves to the Lord"* (2 Corinthians 8:5).

Note from this verse first, ***preeminence of salvation***. Giving ourselves to the Lord is far more important than offering our money. He can survive without our offerings. We can't survive without His Son.

The Macedonians had their priorities in order. If we come before God with open wallets but closed hearts, the effect will be short lived. There's no substitute to offering one's heart to Christ.

Realize too, ***the ultimate recipient of our offerings in the kingdom of God is the Lord Himself***. When collecting money to construct the temple, David said: *"I have seen with joy how willingly your people who are here have given **to you**"* (1 Chronicles 29:17, emphasis added). Speaking of recipients of salvation and eternal life, Jesus said: *"For I was hungry, and you gave Me something to eat; I was thirsty, and you gave Me something to drink; I was a stranger, and you invited Me in . . . to the extent that you did it to one of these brothers of Mine, even the least of them, you did it to Me."* (Matthew 25:35,36,40, emphasis added).

Todd Gaddis

When I was in seminary, a friend of mine suggested we go into the downtrodden sections of Fort Worth and pass out sandwiches to homeless people on the streets. It proved to be a very humbling experience, as I had never done anything like that before. Looking back, I see that it was just as if we were feeding Jesus Himself.

Think of the offering plate as the hand of God the next time it passes your way. Consider that unfortunate person seeking your help as Christ in the flesh.

Those Corinthians were a talented and capable bunch of Christians. As Paul records, they abounded *"In faith and utterance and knowledge and in all earnestness and in the love we inspired in you"* (2 Corinthians 8:7). With that in mind, he challenged them to excel in their giving as well.

The potential of the First century church pales in comparison to what believers today could do if only they could overcome the misconceptions just discussed and embrace kingdom generosity, the model for such a challenge being Jesus Christ Himself. As Paul writes, *"Though He was rich, yet for your sake He became poor, so that you through his poverty might become rich"* (2 Corinthians 8:9). Jesus sacrificed the bliss of heaven by coming to this sin-soaked world in human form. And He didn't stop there. He went on to suffer a humiliating death on a cross between two thieves so that we could share in the riches of His grace. What greater motivation for giving could there be?

David Young tells a story about picking blackberries as he grew up on a farm. With scratched arms and torn pants, he would proudly present his mother with a bucket of his succulent harvest exclaiming, "These are for you." His mom took his generous offering with a smile. She'd wash the berries and then give them back to her son in a bowl with sugar and cream.

God responds to our offerings to Him in much the same way. Whether they be our resources or our very lives, He returns them richer, sweeter and better than they were before.

12

GOD'S MESSENGERS

"For He will give His angels charge concerning you,
To guard you in all your ways"
(Psalm 91:11).

ഇൡ

Global security is huge, especially since 9/11. It's priority #1 publicly and big business privately. Man-made disasters top the list of America's biggest fears. Yet, for all the protection taking place at home and around the world that you see, even more takes place daily that you don't see. And much of it is being provided by angels. They appear throughout Scripture, from Genesis through Revelation. "There are 108 places in the Old Testament where angels are mentioned and 165 places in the New Testament."[1]

Like people, angels are created beings. They speak and express emotion. Unlike people, they don't age. Being neither male nor female, they have no ability to reproduce. Also, they "Have the ability to change their appearance and shuttle in a flash from the capital glory of heaven to earth and back again."[2]

As we explore this topic of angels, let's begin by addressing the question, **"What does the Bible say about them?** First, they are

93

messengers. This comes as no surprise since the word for angel in the original language in both the Old and New Testaments means *messenger.* "In Hebrew, the word "angel" is the same as the name of the last book of the Old Testament, Malachi. That's the Hebrew word for angel. Malachi means my angel, or my messenger. So Malachi was God's messenger."[3]

An angelic messenger spoke to Moses through a burning bush (Exodus 3:2). Later, God sent an angel to lead the Hebrews out of Egypt (Numbers 20:16). God used an angel to direct Phillip to the Ethiopian official (Acts 8:26). As Paul sailed for an uncertain future in Rome, God sent an angel to deliver a message of assurance and encouragement (Acts 27:23-25).

"GOD IS MY STRENGTH"

The main messenger angel in the Bible is Gabriel, whose name means "God is my strength." Gabriel makes four appearances, the most notable being to Mary when he announced the birth of Christ. He said, *"Behold, you will conceive in your womb and bear a son, and you shall name Him Jesus. He will be great and will be called the Son of the Most High; and the Lord God will give Him the throne of His father David; and He will reign over the house of Jacob forever, and His kingdom will have no end"* (Luke 1:31-33). Just prior Gabriel visited Zechariah, foretelling the upcoming birth of John the Baptist (Luke 1:19).

Gabriel's other two appearances in Scripture are in the book of Daniel. On the first occasion, he came to interpret a complex vision the prophet had regarding Israel's enemies and the end times. (Daniel 8:16-26). Later, in response to Daniel's prayer, Gabriel unveils additional prophet insight. (Daniel 9:21-27).

Like messengers, angels also serve as **ministers**. *"Are they (angels) not ministering spirits, sent out to render service for the sake of those who will inherit salvation?"* (Hebrews 1:14).

As ministering servants, observe that angels *provide*. Elijah experienced this when he ran for his life from Jezebel. As the prophet lay sleeping under a tree, an angel came and provided a meal for him. This gave Elijah the strength to embark upon a lengthy journey of 40 days.

The best example of ministering angels in the Bible takes place in the life of Jesus. After being baptized, Jesus underwent intense temptation from Satan, not to mention the fact that he had been fasting for 40 days. Once Satan left Him, *"Angels came and began to minister to Him"* (Matthew 4:11).

The night before He went to the cross, agonizing through prayer in the Garden of Gethsemane, *"An angel from heaven appeared to Him, strengthening Him"* (Luke 22:43). "The Greek word for strengthening is *eniskuo,* which means to make strong inwardly."[4] While the disciples slept through their chance to attend their friend in His time of need, an angel came to assist. Also, had He only commanded it, angels would have come and taken Jesus down from the cross and saved His life. He knew, however, that He must endure such a death in order to provide payment for the sins of mankind.

Three days later, an angel descended from heaven and rolled the stone away from Jesus' grave (Matthew 28:2). Fifty days after that, two men in white clothing, no doubt angels, stood beside Jesus as He ascended back to Heaven (Acts 1:9-11).

Billy Graham writes about the following: During World War II, Captain Eddie Rickenbacker and the rest of the crew of the B-17 in which he was flying ran out of fuel and "ditched" in the Pacific Ocean. For weeks, nothing was heard of him. The newspapers reported his disappearance and across the country thousands of people prayed. Mayor LaGuardia asked the whole city of New York to pray for him. Then, he returned. The Sunday papers headlined the news, and in an article, Captain Rickenbacker told what had happened. "And this part I would hesitate to tell," he wrote, "except that there were six witnesses who saw it with me. A gull came out of nowhere, and lighted on my head—I reached up my hand very gently—I killed him, and then we divided him equally among us. We ate every bit, even the little bones. Nothing ever tasted so good." This gull saved the lives of Rickenbacker and his companions. Years later I asked him to tell me the story personally, because it was through the experience that he came to know Christ. He said, "I have no explanation except that God sent one of His angels to rescue us."[5]

We observe as well that ministering angels in the Bible *protect*. After God banned Adam and Eve from the Garden of Eden, He stationed angels at the tree of life to stand guard (Genesis 3:24). On initial consideration, this may seem like punishment, as if God was barring the way back into paradise. But, it was actually protection. "If Adam and Eve, in their fallen condition, had eaten of that tree, they would have lived forever in their sins. They would have become like the fallen angels, incapable of death and forever locked into the guilt and penalty of their sin."[6]

John Paton was a missionary in the New Hebrides Islands. One night hostile natives surrounded the mission station, intent on burning out the Patons and killing them. Paton and his wife prayed during the terror-filled night that God would deliver them. When daylight came they were amazed to see their attackers leave. A year later, the chief of the tribe was converted to Christ. Remembering what had happened, Paton asked the chief what had kept him from burning down the house and killing them. The chief replied in surprise, "Who were all those men with you there?" Paton knew no men were present, but the chief said he was afraid to attack because he had seen hundreds of big men in shining garments with drawn swords circling the mission station.[7]

When Daniel's friends Shadrach, Meshach, and Abednego were thrown into the blazing furnace, God provided a fourth man, an angel, to rescue them from death. Later, Daniel himself was thrown into a lions' den for failing to bow down to an earthly king. After surviving the night, he said, *"My God sent His angel and shut the lions' mouths and they have not harmed me"* (Daniel 3:25, 6:22).

This account begs the question: Do each of us have a guardian angel to protect us from harm on this fallen earth? After all, the Bible does say, *"He will give His angels charge concerning you, To guard you in all your ways"* (Psalm 91:11). Jesus challenged His listeners to take special care of little children, indicating they have angels in heaven watching over them (Matthew 18:11). Obviously, God stands ready to provide and protect us with angels, yet nowhere in Scripture does it say that every person has a personal angel at their disposal.

"WHO IS LIKE GOD"

Understand, as well, that angels carry out God's *judgment*. This can come as a surprise to those who perceive them as the sweet, chubby little figurines that perch on bookshelves. Yet, often in Scripture they serve in a militant capacity.

Michael, whose name means "who is like God," is the most prominent warrior angel in the Bible. He led the divine forces to wage war and defeat Satan and his henchmen when they were thrown out of Heaven (Revelation 12: 7-8). When an angel was prevented by a demon from delivering a message to Daniel, God sent Michael to defeat the foe. Later in that same book, we learn that Michael stands ready to do battle against God's enemies at the end of time (Daniel 10:13, 12:1).

Although named and most notable, Michael wasn't the only warrior angel in Scripture. During the reign of King Hezekiah, an "angel of the LORD" went out and killed 185,000 enemy soldiers (2 Kings 19:35). When King David defied God, and numbered his troops, God sent a pestilence that killed 70,000 men of Israel. On top of that, the same "angel of the Lord" that killed the Assyrians stood ready to destroy the city of Jerusalem. Only after the King's plea for mercy did God accept David's sacrifice and relent (1 Chronicles 21:15-18). Though many feel these appearances, including those in Daniel, were the pre-incarnate Christ, He nevertheless came in the form of angel.

When Herod Agrippa I, the Judean king who persecuted the church and put James the disciple to death, was addressing his subjects, *"The people kept crying out, 'The voice of a god and not of a man!'"* (Acts 12:22). When the King failed to give glory to God, He was struck by an angel and eaten by worms.

Perhaps the most significant purpose angels have is **praising and glorifying God.** The aged disciple John, exiled on the isle of Patmos, received a vision eventually recorded on the pages of Scripture. On one occasion, he looked and heard the voices of millions of angels as they circled the throne and praised God. Loudly, they sang, *"Worthy is the Lamb, who was slain, to receive power and wealth and wisdom and strength and honor and glory and praise!"* (Revelation 5:11).

There is a branch in the angelic ranks called *seraphim* that have a single item on their job description: praise the character and name of God in heaven "24/7." They appear in the Bible at the call of Isaiah the prophet. Catching a glimpse of the LORD on the throne, Isaiah records these six-winged angels calling out to one another, *"Holy, Holy, Holy, is the LORD of hosts, The whole earth is full of His glory"* (Isaiah 6:3). Similarly, during Ezekiel's commission, as the Spirit lifted him up, he heard, *"Blessed be the glory of the LORD in His place,"* as well as *"The sound of the wings of the living beings touching one another"* (Ezekiel 3:12-13).

At the birth of Jesus, on that first Christmas day, a heavenly host appeared, praising God and saying, *"Glory to God in the highest, And on earth peace among men with whom He is pleased"* (Luke 2:14).

ENTERTAINING ANGELS

Everything written in this chapter up till now points toward our second key question: **"What are angels doing today?"** There's no reason to believe they have not continued to do what the Bible tells us throughout history. In heaven, in addition to their ongoing praise of God, the Bible tells us, *"There is joy in the presence of the angels of God over one sinner who repents* (Luke 15:10). With people being saved on a regular basis, around the clock, throughout the world, we know that keeps them busy.

That's all well and good one might say, but what about their activity on earth? A very reputable and influential man in my young adult life told me of an angel that appeared at the foot of his bed to deliver a word of encouragement at a pivotal point in his life. I've never had that happen and likely you haven't either. Yet, similar reports from around the world surface on a regular basis.

Mining deeper into this question, let's contrast and compare *the role of angels to that of the Holy Spirit.* "Some people confuse angels with the Holy Spirit, yet their makeup and job description differ greatly. The over-arching contrast is that the Holy Spirit is *Creator* and angels are *created.* Whereas the Holy Spirit indwells people, angels do not. Possessing the attributes of God, the Holy Spirit can be everywhere at once and should be an object of our worship. "Angels are mightier than men, but they are not gods and do not possess the attributes of the Godhead."[8] They can only be one place at a time and should not be an object worship.

Obviously, both the Holy Spirit and angels help carry out God's perfect plans. There are times when you won't know whether an angel or the Spirit is at work. You "Can be sure, however, that there is no contradiction or competition between God the Holy Spirit and God's command of the angelic hosts."[9]

In a general sense, working omnipotently, the Holy Spirit works as a restrainer of evil in our world. The Bible tells of a time, before the Second Coming of Christ, when this restrainer is removed and the anti-Christ is revealed (2 Thessalonians 2:7,8).

Angels perform a similar function, **battling demons in spiritual warfare.** According to Scripture, *"Our struggle is not against flesh and blood, but against the rulers, against the powers, against the world forces of this darkness, against the spiritual forces of wickedness in the heavenly places"* (Ephesians 6:12). Recall from chapter 4 that one-third of the angels in heaven were cast out along with Lucifer. He became Satan and they became demons, these "rulers, powers, and spiritual forces of wickedness" that make it their number one priority to discourage, defeat, and destroy Christians.

Of course, we have the Holy Spirit within and around us to help in our fight against the devil. As the Bible says, *'Greater is He who is in you than he who is in the world"* (1 John 4:4). In fact, Jesus already won the war against him by giving His life on the cross and rising from the grave. But, until final defeat, the enemy *"Prowls around like a roaring lion, seeking someone to devour"* (1 Peter 5:8). Thankfully, even though we don't see it happening, angels continually battle and defeat Satan's henchmen on a regular basis.

Finally, **angels stand ready to play a significant role in the End Times.** Angels will assist in the tribulation events and accompany the Lord when He returns to the earth. According to John's vision of the Second Coming, a heavenly host of angels, *"armies which are in heaven, clothed in fine linen, white and clean, were following Him on white horses"* (Revelation 19:14).

In addition to following Jesus, these armies will assist Him in the battle at Armageddon. At this time, an angel will proclaim to the birds in the sky, *"Come, assemble for the great supper of God'"* (Revelation 19:17). Not to be confused with the marriage supper of the Lamb (Revelation 19:9), which will be a celebration of saints in heaven, this great supper of God will be a dinner commemorating God's victory over the pagan armies on earth, one after which birds from the sky will feast upon their fallen bodies. After that, angels will help bind Satan in preparation for Christ's millennial reign.

Although you should never worship angels, eagerly anticipate uniting with them in heaven and standing with them in the final days to come. In the meantime, *"Do not neglect to show hospitality to strangers, for by this some have entertained angels without knowing it"* (Hebrews 13:2).

Todd Gaddis

13

"IT SURE IS HOT DOWN HERE!"

"I am in agony in this flame"
(Luke 16:24).

✧

A man traveled from Chicago to Key West for a vacation. His wife was away on business and planned to fly down the next day to meet him. When he arrived, the man e-mailed his wife to inform her that he made it safely. Unfortunately, he mistyped her address and the message ended up going to a woman whose husband had just passed away.

The grieving widow opened her e-mail, read the message, screamed, and then passed out cold. Rushing into the room, the woman's daughter discovered this note on the computer monitor. "My darling wife: Just checked in. Everything is prepared for your arrival tomorrow. Looking forward to being with you again. Your loving husband. P.S. Sure is hot down here!"

I enjoy getting a chuckle out of stories like this one, but the stark reality is hell is no laughing matter. It's a real place reserved for those who reject God's offer of eternal life through His Son Jesus—the default destination for those who simply stroll apathetically through life, failing to find the answer for the problem of sin in their lives.

In my very first week as a new pastor I received a call of complaint from an over-protective mother. I brought up the issue of hell in Vacation Bible School and one of the girls present went home scared. Please understand that it's never my practice to frighten kids, or adults for that matter. However, I don't intend to shy away from Biblical truth either. I preach and teach about hell because Jesus talked about it, often in fact.

There are three different Greek words that translate into the English word hell. *Tartaros,* which appears only once in the New Testament (2 Peter 2:4), "is a place of confinement for the rebellious angels until the time of their judgment."[1] *Geena*, or *Gehenna* is rendered "hell" twelve times, eleven of which come from the lips of Jesus Himself.[2] This is a permanent place of punishment, the eternal lake of fire, the second death referred to in Revelation 20.

The word used for hell in our central text for this chapter (read Luke 16:19-31) is *Hades,* which appears ten times in the New Testament. "It is not the final destiny of those who die having rejected Christ, but a place of torment until they are resurrected to stand before the great white throne judgment" (Revelation 20:13-15).[3] Please understand, this does not suggest a period of purgatory, or an opportunity for second chance—but rather a place where lost souls suffer in torment until permanent judgment is carried out following the millennial reign of Christ. Grasp the following truths about Hades that will no doubt carry over into Gehenna as well.

"SON, REMEMBER"

Those in hell will retain their memory of things that happened on earth, as indicated by Abraham's words to the rich man, *"Child, remember that during your life you received your good things, and likewise Lazarus bad things"* (Luke 16:25). What else did the rich man do but reflect upon how foolish he had been, becoming so enamored with his wealth yet failing to acknowledge the One who had blessed him with it. Forever he would replay in his mind the times he had walked by Lazarus without so much as glancing his way. He even remembered his five brothers that were headed for his dreadful, deadly destination (Luke 16:28).

I believe with all my heart that at this very moment occupants of hell are remembering the multiple opportunities they had to repent of their sins and submit to Christ. Millions upon millions are recalling the times they felt the conviction of the Holy Spirit but would not humble themselves before God.

Hard-hearted husbands regretfully reflect upon the times they turned a deaf ear to their wives' pleas to attend church with her and the children. Those who encountered death unexpectedly, some perhaps in their younger years, replay repeatedly every single opportunity they had to get saved. The person who said, "I'm not ready now but maybe someday" will be constantly reminded that someday never came. Likewise, the rich man has eternity to remember his spiritual failures.

Next, note that **hell is a place of perpetual agony.** In a pitiful appeal to Abraham, the rich man said, *"Have mercy on me . . . I am in agony in this flame"* (Luke 16:24). Is Jesus referring to literal flames? We can't say for sure. Certainly, He described hell as such on multiple occasions. He warned of *"the fiery hell, the furnace of fire,"* and *"hell . . . the unquenchable the fire"* (Matthew 5:22, 13:42, Mark 9:44). John writes of death and Hades being thrown into *"the lake of fire"* after the millennial reign of Christ (Revelation 20:14).

A scoffer might say, "It couldn't be actual fire because those present would be burned up in a matter of minutes." Remember the burning bush that Moses saw in the desert. The Bible says that, *"the bush was burning with fire, yet the bush was not consumed"* (Exodus 3:2). If

God performed such a phenomenon with a plant on this earth, He could certainly do it with people in hell.

Even if the flames aren't literally there, the physical misery will be. And yet, it pales in comparison to the mental and emotional anguish that hell's occupants endure. As Jesus hung dying on the cross, he cried out, *"My God, my God, why have you forsaken me?"* (Matthew 27:46). The physical pain of being nailed to the cross meant little to Him compared to the agony being separated from the Father and becoming sin for us. The spiritual agony in hell overshadows anything physically endured.

Observe also that **hell means eternal separation,** as described by the following:

Separation from God — *"Between us and you there is a great chasm fixed,"* said Abraham, *"so that those who wish to come over from here to you will not be able, and that none may cross over from there to us"*(Luke 16:26).

Thankfully, for those still alive on earth, there is a way to cross the chasm. Yet it can't happen as a result of our own efforts. Rather it's the sacrifice of Christ that allows sinful man to connect with a perfect God. If you've not done so, make the connection now by receiving His offer of salvation and forgiveness. Otherwise, you're doomed to an eternity of separation after you die.

Separation from people — Lazarus was carried by angels to Abraham's side after his death. We learn of no such welcome for the rich man.

"SOLITARY CONFINEMENT"

I've heard it said about rebellious unbelievers that they don't dread the prospects of hell, as long as they can party with their rebellious friends. I've got news for them—nothing could be further from the truth. While Christians can anticipate joyous fellowship—

with Jesus, angels and other saints in their life to come—the unsaved can expect nothing but aloneness and confinement.

I toured a prison recently and was shown the tiny, isolation cells reserved for inmates who disobey certain rules. For up to 30 days, they remain isolated from the rest of the prison community without media, interaction with inmates or visits from family members. Obviously, this is viewed as extreme punishment, otherwise, why would it serve to deter bad behavior? Likewise, banishment and separation is part of the extreme sentence that awaits unbelievers.

Hell is characterized by unending hopelessness – What more than hope keeps us going on this fallen, sin-soaked planet? As the rain pours down, we anticipate sunny days. As the winter winds blow and trees stand gray and bare, we can anticipate the warmth and green that await. We struggle through the fever and pain of the flu, knowing that recovery is just days away. The loneliness of time spent apart from those we love gets quickly pushed aside by the thought of seeing them soon. We toil away at difficult and demanding jobs day after day, week after week, month after month, eagerly anticipating a much-needed vacation or well-deserved retirement. While still alive on earth, nearly everything can be taken from us but hope. In hell, however, even that gets stripped away.

In 1927, the Coast Guard cutter USS *Paulding* rammed a Navy S-4 submarine off the coast of Massachusetts.[4] The crew of the vessel became trapped in an underwater prison of death. Great lengths were taken to rescue those on board, but ultimately, they all failed. Near the end of the tragedy, a diver heard tapping on the steel wall of the vessel. He placed his helmet next to the side of the sunken sub and recognized Morse code. One of the doomed sailors repeatedly spelled out the question, "Is . . . there . . . any . . . hope?"[5]

For the rich man, there was no hope—and he likely knew it. He asks for water, and even requests that Lazarus be allowed to go warn his brothers; yet we never hear a plea for release or a second chance.

He had nothing else to do but remember, agonize, suffer through separation, and drown in hopelessness. Ponder again this unmistakable truth—hell is real.

Finally, **possession of worldly wealth increases a person's chance of going to hell.** The rich man in our story *"habitually dressed in purple and fine linen, joyously living in splendor every day"* (Luke 16:19). Obviously, his possessions did not automatically seal his dreadful fate. His prosperity, however, created a false sense of security. Why depend on God when he had everything a person could want at his disposal? Accumulation and the distractions that go along with it prohibited his necessary preparation for the future. As the Word says, *"It is easier for a camel to go through the eye of a needle than for a rich man to enter the kingdom of heaven"* (Mark 10:25).

"YOU STILL LACK ONE THING"

Jesus made this comment at the end of an encounter with a rich young ruler when the man approached the Lord and asked Him the way to eternal life. After they discussed keeping the commandments, Jesus said to him, *"You still lack one thing. Sell everything you have and give to the poor, and you will have treasure in heaven. Then come, follow me"* (Luke 18:22).

Certainly, the Lord wasn't suggesting that entrance into heaven could be earned. He probed for a willing spirit and at the same time exposed the barrier that stood between the man and eternal life. Unfortunately, the young man rejected the Lord's offer and headed down a path toward hell because of his love affair with worldly wealth.

Another parable from Jesus illustrated this claim. The ground of a certain rich man produced such a bountiful harvest that he ran out of room to store his crops. Agonizing over his good fortune, he said, *"This is what I'll do. I will tear down my barns and build bigger ones, and there I will store all my grain and my goods. And I'll say to myself, 'You have plenty of good things laid up for many years. Take life easy; eat, drink and be merry'"* (Luke 12:18,19). Upon hearing the man's plan, God responded, *"You fool! This very night your life will be demanded from you"* (Luke 12:20). Earlier in the Lord's ministry he proclaimed, *"Woe to you who are rich, for you have already received your comfort. Woe to you who are well fed now, for you will go hungry"* (Luke 6:24,25).

Years ago, a policeman issued a citation to a woman in New York. When the officer handed the ticket through the lady's window, she snapped it out of his hand and said, "You can go straight to hell!" Thus, the policeman took her to court. When the case went up for review, the judge dismissed the complaint about the woman's language, saying, "It wasn't a command, or a wish, but a statement of fact, for going to hell is a possibility."[5]

I don't condone the woman's vulgarity and also have concerns about the ruling. However, the statement is 100 per-cent on target. *Going to hell is a possibility.* For the rich man, it was a reality. However, it's certainly not a necessity. Heaven, which we move on to learn more about now, is a much better alternative.

Todd Gaddis

14

SOMETHING BETTER

"We have a building from God, a house not
made with hands, eternal in the heavens"
(2 Corinthians 5:1).

&⊃⊂ℬ

The Associated Press named Pepper Martin their athlete of the year in 1931. The Oklahoma native and right-handed center fielder batted .500, stole five bases, scored five runs, and played excellent defense to lead his St. Louis Cardinals to a World Series victory over the Philadelphia Athletics.

After the seventh and decisive game, the press cornered him for an interview. In the midst of celebration, a reporter asked, "Pepper, now that you have won the World Series single-handedly, what do you want more than anything else in the world?"

Following a pondering pause, he startled them with his answer. "Above everything else in the world I want to go to heaven." As the group of reporters laughed, a serious Martin peered into their eyes and said, "What's so funny about that? I *do* want above everything else to go to heaven."[1] And who wouldn't, based on everything the Bible tells us about how wonderful this "paradise" is going to be?

"HE'S PREPARED A PLACE"

Those commended for their faith in Hebrews 11 did not receive fulfillment of God's promise to them while still alive because He *"had provided* **something better** *for us, so that apart from us they would not be made perfect"* (Hebrews 11:40, emphasis added). That "something better" is **heaven**, which can first be described as **a created place.**

Focusing on the word "created," realize that there has never been a time that God wasn't. He was, is, and always will be. The Word says, *"In the beginning God created the heavens and the earth"* (Genesis 1:1). This clearly indicates that God was around before heaven ever came into being.

Consider, too, the term "place." Heaven is anything but some mystical mist floating around in the clouds or among the stars. Just hours before His crucifixion, the Lord comforted His disciples by assuring them He was going to prepare a place for them (John 14:2).

According to the Bible, special saints had the opportunity to gaze upon a portion of its mystery. Isaiah caught a vision of the Lord encircled by angels while being commissioned into prophetic service (Isaiah 6:1). Stephen saw heaven open and Jesus at the Father's right hand just moments before his death. John the Revelator viewed and recorded evidence of a literal, observable, tangible location.

These and other Scriptures indicate also that **heaven is the current home of God, His son Jesus, angels, and all believers who have died up to this point**. God is spirit and does not need a specific place to dwell. Yet, we know He's there because the Word says so. Solomon prayed to God, *"Hear in heaven Your dwelling place"* (1 Kings 8:30).

Not only does God reside there, but Jesus as well. After His death, burial and resurrection, Christ entered *"into heaven itself, now to appear in the presence of God for us"* (Hebrews 9:24). Speaking before a group of children, Jesus said, *"See that you do not despise one of these little ones, for I say to you that their angels in heaven continually see the face of My*

Father who is in heaven" (Matthew 18:10). Paul told the church at Corinth that to be absent from the body is to be present with the Lord. (2 Corinthians 5:8).

Next, **heaven hosts peerless, perpetual praise.** So much of our worship on earth is flawed. We honor God with our lips but our hearts are far from Him. (Isaiah 29:13). We come to Him in praise despite unconfessed sin in our lives. Our minds are prone to wander. Those who don't know Jesus sing along as if they did. Too often, our times of worship are too predictable, scripted, and brief.

Such is not the case in heaven. In His vision from the isle of Patmos, John saw living creatures, or angels, at God's throne saying: *"HOLY, HOLY, HOLY is THE LORD GOD ALMIGHTY, WHO WAS AND WHO IS AND WHO IS TO COME"* (Revelation 4:8). Later, the beloved disciple saw a countless multitude standing at the throne before the Lamb crying out, *"Salvation to our God, who sits on the throne, and to the Lamb"* (Revelation 7:10).

"SOMETHING TO SING ABOUT"

The book *Psalms of the Heart* contains the story of two missionaries who traveled to southern Mexico to work among the Chol Indians. Among other ministries, they labored 25 years to translate the New Testament into the local language. Today, more than 12,000 make up the Chol Christian Community—which, by the way, is financially self-supporting.

What's most amazing is that when the missionaries arrived, the locals didn't even know how to sing. Upon their conversion, however, the Christians in the tribe became known as "the singers." "They love to sing now," said author George Sweeting, "because they have something to sing about."[2] If you know Jesus as Savior, you too, have something to sing about.

I look over my congregation each Sunday and see so many with mouths tightly closed during our songs. You say, "I'm one of those, Todd. I sing horribly. My voice is monotone. On top of that, I don't like those choruses. Why, I even saw some people raise their hands! I'll start singing when we get rid of the drums and the choir starts wearing robes again."

Praise God these won't be issues in heaven. Instead of feeling self-conscious and looking around to see what others are doing, we'll focus on the One worthy of our honor and worship.

In addition to its praise, **heaven is a place of unprecedented beauty.** A little girl and her father were out for a walk in the country after dark. There were no streetlights, auto headlights, bright signs, etc.—nothing but a deep blue velvet sky studded with an array of shining stars.

"Daddy," the daughter said, "if the wrong side of heaven is so beautiful, what do you think the right side will be like?"

Jesus assured the repentant thief on the cross beside Him, *"Today you shall be with Me in Paradise"* (Luke 23:43). "This Persian word meaning 'garden' is used in the Old Testament of a number of gardens. Specifically important is its use for the Garden of Eden." [3] Obviously, Christ was pointing to the beautiful surroundings they would soon enjoy. In his view of heaven, John saw beautiful stone, a rainbow like an emerald in appearance, a sea of glass like crystal and elders with golden crowns on their heads. (Revelation 4:3-6).

I once traveled with my family through several western states. I observed many breathtaking sights, my favorite being the Grand Teton Mountains in northwestern Wyoming. I stood on the patio of the Jackson Lake Lodge transfixed, gazing at the jagged, snowcapped range that sprang forth from a blanket of green marshland.

If we can have such pinch-me-to-see-if-I'm-really-awake encounters on this fallen planet, what more must await us in Heaven? Heaven will contain a continual source of surreal sights and sounds—none of which we have been privy to here on earth.

"REST FROM YOUR LABOR"

Adding to the bliss is **the rest we'll experience in heaven**. Since the Fall, man has had to obtain food by the sweat of his brow. (Genesis 3:19). I believe this curse extends and applies, in general, to survival/making a living.

Everywhere I go, I see people burning candles at both ends. Family, career, and community responsibilities are smothering us. Church can exhaust us if we're not careful. I know many people who've literally worn themselves out by taking care of others. Heaven provides relief from such toil. In the midst of one of John's visions, a voice said, *"Write, 'Blessed are the dead who die in the Lord from now on!'"* *'Yes,' says the Spirit, 'so that they my rest from their labors'"* (Revelation 14:13, emphasis added). This is not to say that saints will spend eternity lounging on clouds, in a constant state of retirement and inactivity. There will be lots to "do" in heaven. Fortunately, we won't wear ourselves out in the process.

Finally, **heaven as it currently exists is a temporary place**. This might raise a few eyebrows, since we're used to thinking of heaven as eternal and endless. Yet, as bestselling author Randy Alcorn states and Scripture affirms, "The intermediate Heaven is *not* our final destination. Though it will be a wonderful place, the intermediate Heaven is not the place we were made for—the place God promises to refashion for us to live in forever."[4]

For the believer, intermediate heaven serves as a stopping over point between death and Christ's return to the earth. This is called the disembodied state. When we die, our spirits depart our temporal earth suits and go into the presence of the Lord. Before Jesus died on the cross he called out loudly, "Father, into your hands I commit my spirit" (Luke 23:46). Why did He not say, *"Father, into your hands I commit my body?"* The reason is, His body was taken down from the cross and placed in the tomb. Three days later He came forth from the grave with a glorified, resurrection body. As Christians, we'll have to wait until the Second Coming to receive our resurrection bodies.

Note from our central text that Paul said, *"We . . . would prefer to be away from the body and at home with the Lord"* (2 Corinthians 5:8). The phrase "home with the Lord" refers to a disembodied state in the intermediate heaven with Jesus.

This discussion begs these questions: First, with our earthly shells buried in a grave, *what kind of bodies will we possess during the intermediate state?* Although the Bible doesn't address this inquiry directly, answers are implied. When Lazarus, the poor man in chapter four, died, he was carried to Abraham's side. The rich man in hell asked if Lazarus' finger could be dipped in water. Obviously, "side" and "finger" allude to some type of physical presence. In John's vision, he witnessed martyrs under the altar in white robes (Revelation 6:11). What good would a robe be without some type of body to put under it?

Also, *will we recognize one another in intermediate heaven, during our disembodied state?* Although we still won't have glorified, resurrected bodies, I believe God has provided a means for us to know one another. At the Transfiguration, Moses and Elijah appeared in recognizable, physical form to Jesus, Peter, James, and John. Although one could argue that this Old Testament pair was given some type of temporary body for their return to earth, it's more likely that they maintained some type of incarnate presence, one that they maintain to this day.

Billy Graham tells the story of his grandmother's final moments on earth. While in her dying state, "She sat up in her bed, smiled and said, 'I see Jesus, and He has His hand outstretched to me. And there's Ben and he has both of his eyes and both of his legs.' My grandfather had lost a leg and an eye at Gettysburg."[5]

In Valladolid, Spain, where Christopher Columbus died in 1506, stands a monument commemorating the great discoverer. Perhaps the most fascinating feature of the memorial is a statue of a lion destroying one of the Latin words that helped make up Spain's motto for centuries. Before Columbus launched out, the Spaniards thought they had reached the earth's outer limits. Thus, their motto proclaimed "Ne Plus Ultra," which means "No More Beyond." The word being stripped away by the lion is "ne" or "no," making it read "Plus Ultra." Columbus proved that there was indeed "more beyond."[6]

Life on this fallen planet is but a mere dot on the radar screen of eternity. There's "Plus Ultra." Something better, a paradise of beauty, rest, praise and untainted fellowship awaits those born again.

Todd Gaddis

15

"I SHALL RETURN"

"For the Lord Himself will descend from heaven…"
(1 Thessalonians 4:16).

ങ്ങ

In an early stage in World War II, General Douglas MacArthur and his army endured one of the lowest times in American history. When the Japanese attacked the Philippines, his isolated forces fought valiantly, but eventually withdrew to Bataan Peninsula, where they resisted bravely for four months. Later, in March of 1942, President Roosevelt ordered the controversial General to relocate to Australia and command Southwest Pacific Allied forces.

After arriving "Down Under" and traveling by rail through the outback, he spoke of his reluctance to leave his men and also made this famous promise from Terowie, South Australia: "I came out of Bataan and *I shall return*." On October 20, 1944, his troops invaded Leyte and six months later the Philippines celebrated liberation. He departed in defeat but kept his promise and returned in victory.

A few weeks after the resurrection, a small band of believers met with Jesus in Jerusalem. After a going away meal, the Lord reminded them of the promised arrival of the Holy Spirit, and then ascended to

Heaven. As the disciples watched His departure, two angels appeared and said, *"Why do you stand looking into the sky? This Jesus, who has been taken from you into heaven, will come in just the same way as you have watched Him go into heaven"* (Acts 1:11).

"A THIEF IN THE NIGHT"

A basic belief in the Christian faith, the Second Coming is mentioned over 300 times in the New Testament alone. And while many are obsessed with *when* this event will occur, I'd like to come at it from the angle of *how* and *why*.

First, Jesus will return **suddenly.** He said to His disciples during Passion Week, *"Therefore be on the alert, for you do not know which day your Lord is coming"* (Matthew 24:42). Later, He told John in the Patmos vision, *"Behold, I am coming like a thief. Blessed is the one who stays awake and keeps his clothes, so that he will not walk about naked and men will not see his shame"* (Revelation 16:15). Paul voiced the same warning: *"You yourselves know that the day of the Lord will come just like a thief in the night"* (1 Thessalonians 5:2).

I'll never forget walking into the church I served several years ago, surprised and angered to discover that the door to my office had been busted open. Screws and springs from the doorknob lay strewn across the floor. Thieves had broken in through a window during the night and stolen a television, VCR, and sound equipment. If we had known they were coming, we would have installed a security system or arranged for someone to stand watch. They entered the building unexpectedly and we were unprepared.

Such will be the scenario when Jesus makes His earthly return. While believers will rise to meet their Savior in the air, the unredeemed will remain behind, unprepared. I implore you to *"Be ready; for the Son of Man is coming at an hour when you do not think He will"* (Matthew 24:44).

Yet, understand: a *sudden* return does not mean a *subtle* return. *Quickly* won't be *quietly*. God's Son came silently and humbly the first time to a sleepy village outside Jerusalem. Except for a few shepherds and magi, everyone missed it. Such will not be the case when He reappears **gloriously**, as the following descriptions indicate.

- **Clouds will transport Him from Heaven to earth. (Matthew 24:30)**

- **The archangel will announce His coming. (1 Thessalonians 4:16)**

- **Angels and fire will accompany His entourage. (2 Thessalonians 1:7)**

- **A cavalry of angels and saints will join Him. (Revelation 19:14)**

Taking on the throne of Israel, King David proceeded to conquer Jerusalem and rout the Philistines. He then brought the ark of God to the capital city. Returning to Jerusalem victoriously with the ark, David and the house of Israel joyously commemorated the triumph. *"Dancing before the LORD with all his might . . . with shouting and the sound of the trumpet"* (2 Samuel 6:14,15), the people gloriously celebrated. Likewise, Christ's return will involve majestic extravaganza.

Observe that He will come back **victoriously** as well. As the great tribulation draws to its furious and fatal close, with Jerusalem's future hanging in the balance and the Antichrist creating continual deception and destruction, the Lord will answer the prayers of a repentant remnant by coming to launch a final assault of war and judgment. *"From His mouth comes a sharp sword, so that with it He may strike down the nations, and He will rule them with a rod of iron; and He treads the wine press of the fierce wrath of God, the Almighty"* (Revelation 19:15).

Kings of the earth join the beast in a hopeless attempt to battle Christ on the plain of Armageddon —to no avail. The enemy will suffer a blistering defeat. Blood will flow out of the great winepress of God's wrath, *"Up to the horses' bridles, for a distance of two hundred miles"* (Revelation 14:20). Ultimately, the beast and false prophet will be thrown into a fiery lake of burning sulfur.

This image of Jesus bothers some people. They would rather view Him as the gentle, pacifistic, peace lover who remained silent and turned the other cheek before his accusers. Others ask, "How could a loving God put His stamp of approval on any form of war?" Obviously, He doesn't relish it. Yet times arise when no other choice exists.

The Old Testament tells of many battles between God's chosen and their enemies, ones in which He intervened and numerous lives were lost. Abraham, Joshua, Gideon, Saul, and David are just a few of the many who commanded soldiers in conquests over their enemies. Yet nothing to date can compare to Jesus spearheading the ultimate victory.

"GOD WITH A FACE"

Finally, see that Jesus will return to the earth to establish **heavenly conditions**, the first being the literal *revelation of Himself.* Currently, the Holy Spirit takes the place of the bodily presence of Jesus on this planet, since the Lord sits at the right hand of the Father. Only those He encountered during His earthly ministry and the saints in heaven have had the privilege of seeing Him up close and personal. When He comes again, however, believers throughout all ages will be in on His appearing. As John writes, *"We know that when He appears, we will be like Him, because we will see him just as He is"* (1 John 3:2).

An African, who wore around his neck an amulet, was detained as a prisoner of war. When this charm was taken from him, he became distraught and begged that it be returned to him. He valued the lucky piece so much that he was willing to sacrifice his right hand for it. It meant as much to him as life itself.

It turned out to be a very simple little object—a small, leather case enclosing a slip of paper on which was written one word: *God*. He believed that wearing this charm protected him from evil. When it was given back to him, he was so thrilled that tears streamed down his face. Falling to the ground, he kissed the feet of the man who returned it.

The Second Coming will be so much more than a slip of paper with "God" inscribed on it. God in the flesh, the Son of God, will make a personal and permanent appearance.

The second heavenly condition established by His coming is *the binding of Satan.* Although the Antichrist and false prophet have been thrown into a lake of fire by this time, Satan remains alive and active. But then, God arranges his imprisonment. As mentioned in a previous chapter, an angel *"Threw him into the abyss, and shut it and sealed it over him, so that he would not deceive the nations any longer, until the thousand years were completed"* (Revelation 20:3).

Two phrases from this verse deserve special attention. First, pay heed to "the nations," which introduces an intriguing but confusing dilemma. Although there are those that feel that only believers will be alive at this stage in history, I believe this designation refers to lost that are still alive after Christ's return. The fact that Jesus achieves victory over His enemies doesn't mean He has destroyed them all, at least not at this point. After all, if only believers remain to populate the earth, who are "the deceived"?

Some think those deluded are offspring of believers born between the Second Coming and Satan's ultimate demise. I believe this cannot be the case, since this violates what Jesus taught about procreation and the resurrected body (Luke 20:35,36). The lost, however, will continue to multiply because they do not possess glorified bodies.

The term "thousand years," which appears six times in as many verses (Revelation 20: 2-7), merits detailed discussion as well. Many call this period the "millennium" or "millennial reign of Christ," staunchly believing that it refers to a literal thousand years. But, remember, much of Revelation is written in apocalyptic language, where numbers often possess symbolic meaning (Revelation 5:11, 11:4, 14:1).

As George Ladd states, "It is difficult to understand the thousand years for which he was bound with strict literalness in view of the obvious symbolic use of numbers in the Revelation. A thousand equals the third power of ten—an ideal time. While we need not take it literally, the thousand years does appear to represent a real period of time, however long or short it may be."[1] I am in complete agreement with Ladd. If this unsettles you, consider the words of the apostle Peter: *"With the Lord one day is like a thousand years, and a thousand years like one day"* (2 Peter 3:8).

No one but God knows for sure. What we can confirm, though, is that after the thousand years, *"Satan will be released from his prison, and will come out to deceive the nations which are in the four corners of the earth"* (Revelation 20:7,8). This short-lived freedom continues until he is eliminated for good as fire from heaven destroys the fallen ones and Satan himself finally and permanently joins the beast and false prophet in the lake of burning sulfur (Revelation 20:10).

"NEVER GIVE UP HOPE"

Lastly, this heavenly condition involves *physical renovation and spiritual renewal*. Although this won't be equal to the new heaven and new earth that follows the Great White Throne Judgment (see chapter 18), it will be a vast improvement over what remains after the tribulation. As a result of this *"Time of distress such as never occurred since there was a nation until that time*" (Daniel 12:1), the following will take place:

- **One half of the world's population will be killed.**

- **The earth will be severely damaged by man-made and natural disasters.**

- **Earthquakes, disease, and warfare will abound.**

- **Humanity will border on extinction.**

Fortunately, this will all turn around quickly once Jesus' millennial reign gets underway. First, the earth will undergo a physical transformation. As the Word states, *"The land will be changed into a plain . . . Jerusalem will rise"* (Zechariah 14:10).

Societal transformation will take place as well. Jerusalem, now the most important city on earth, will experience a rise in population to go along with its increased elevation (Zechariah 14:11). Under divine protection, children will once again play in the streets as the elderly sit and visit together (Zechariah 8:4-5). God's people will experience increased prosperity, because *"The wealth of all the nations will be gathered, gold and silver garments in great abundance "* (Zechariah 14:14).

Thankfully, people will continue to be saved. Scripture tells us, *"So many peoples and mighty nations will come to seek the LORD of hosts in Jerusalem and to entreat the favor of the LORD"* (Zechariah 8:22). Best of all, Jesus, now reigning on earth as King, will be worshipped as never before (Zechariah 14:16).

For the past fifteen years, my church has been involved in an extensive renovation project. Although the building is basically the same structurally, we are thoroughly enjoying our elevator, new windows, sheet rocked walls (versus the old concrete blocks), fresh paint, new carpet, tile floors, brightened entrances, updated lighting, etc. Likewise, believers will enjoy a renovated earth under the millennial headship of Christ, since He'll return not only as redeemer, but rebuilder as well.

In 1914, English explorer Sir Ernest Shackleton led an expedition to the South Pole. In a time of frozen frenzy, he was forced to leave most his men stranded on Elephant Island while he journeyed for help. Safely reaching South Georgia Island, he secured another ship and returned to rescue his crew. Nearing Elephant Island again, he found an opening in the ice and went ashore. With little time to spare, he boarded his men and slipped out before the ice became impassable.

When the jubilation subsided, Sir Ernest asked one of the crew, "How did it happen you were packed and ready for my coming and that you were standing on the shore ready to leave at a moment's notice?"

The man replied, "When you left you said you would come back for us, and we never gave up hope."[2]

Don't give up hope! Jesus promised He'd come again and He will. In the meantime, make the most of every opportunity to grow in Him and help others on their journeys as well.

16

WORTHLESS STUBBLE OR COSTLY STONES?

"We must all appear before the
judgment seat of Christ"
(2 Corinthians 5:10).

&)CB

Once upon a time in a western town, a horse bolted away pulling a wagon that carried a small boy. Spotting the child in peril, a daring young man risked death by stopping the runaway buggy. Sadly, the rescued child grew into a lawless adult. Eventually, he ended up before a judge, awaiting sentence for a serious crime. Recognizing the judge as the man who saved his life years before, the prisoner begged for mercy on the basis of that earlier experience. The judge's reply stymied the plea: "Young man, on that day I was your savior; today, I am your judge, and I sentence you to be hanged."[1]

Two thousand years ago, Jesus Christ came to this planet as Savior. Next time, He'll come back as Judge. The thought of Christ returning gloriously and victoriously brings about a mood of celebration. However, the idea of Him coming again judiciously instills a certain amount of apprehension, and so it should.

For years, I viewed final justice as a single event. Deeper study, however, helped me realize that the Bible speaks of two distinct end time judgments. Here, we'll explore what's in store for believers following *the first resurrection* (Revelation 20:4). This time is referred to as the Judgment Seat of Christ, which will take place once the Lord returns. The next chapter deals with the horror that awaits those who reject Jesus Christ as savior.

The Bible says: *"For we must all appear before the judgment seat of Christ, so that each one may be recompensed for his deeds in the body, according to what he has done, whether good or bad"* (2 Corinthians 5:10). The word in the original language translated "judgment seat" is *bema*, which "Refers to a raised platform on which a ruler or judge would sit to pronounce his decree."[2] On trial for his faith in Corinth, Paul was brought before the judgment seat (Acts 18:12).

Likewise, at the Second Coming, believers will appear on a much grander stage before their Savior. But before we explore what the Judgment Seat of Christ *is*, understand what it *is not*. This judgment *does not determine whether a person gains entrance into heaven.* That issue has already been resolved, and is based on whether the person accepted Christ while alive on earth. Also, *this will not be a time of punishment for sins.* Christ bore punishment for our sins on Calvary's cross two thousand years ago. *"As far as the east is from the west, So far has he removed our transgressions from us"* (Psalm 103:12). God will never dig up and hold sins against us that He's already forgiven and forgotten. What He will do, however, on this critical occasion is recognize and react to our lifetime attitudes and actions.

"NOTHING IS HIDDEN"

See first, this will be a time of **exposure.** Jesus said, *"For nothing is hidden, except to be revealed; nor has anything been secret, but that it would come to light"* (Mark 4:22), a claim that I believe makes specific reference to the Second Coming. Paul wrote that God will one day *"Judge the secrets of men through Jesus Christ"* (Romans 2:16).

When my twenty-something daughter was a toddler, she swallowed a curtain hook. We took her to the hospital and they immediately performed an X- ray, which showed the metal object caught in her throat. The curtain hook was exposed, brought to light and then removed.

Likewise, for believers, the return of Christ will trigger a coming to light, a time of exposure and accountability, and especially a true evaluation of our *deeds.* According to Paul, our efforts and accomplishments will be shown for what they are at the Second Coming. Some Christians build their foundations on wood, hay and straw (1 Corinthians 3:12-13). These deeds may stand the test of time, generating a position in the church and accolades among peers. Ultimately, they will not survive judgment seat scrutiny.

According to the Bible, this time of evaluation will also include accountability for our *words.* Jesus said, *"Every careless word that people speak, they shall give an accounting for it in the day of judgment"* (Matthew 12:36). I sometimes feel awkward when people start recording on their phones around me, knowing that every word is being picked up and preserved. Yet, what's that compared to God's cosmic recorder that logs a lifetime of conversations?

Not only will our actions and words be judged, but the *motives* behind them as well. When the Lord comes, He *"Will both bring to light the things hidden in the darkness and disclose the motives of men's hearts"* (1 Corinthians 4:5).

Sometimes, people join churches for enhanced social status or increased business opportunity. Some make sizable monetary contributions to bask in the publicity and notoriety. Others seek visibility and leadership to feed a hungry ego. These are the kinds of things that will be laid bare at the return of Christ.

This time of judgment also involves **loss.** As stated, the quality of a person's work will be shown for what it is. Speaking symbolically,

Paul wrote: *"It is to be revealed with fire"* (1 Corinthians 3:13). If our contribution to the Kingdom amounts to nothing more than wood, hay and straw, what else can we expect to survive God's flame besides ashes? And, as the Bible says, one whose foundation is burned up *"will suffer loss"* (1 Corinthians 3:15).

Does this refer to a loss of salvation? Certainly, not! As already stated, this judgment does not determine salvation. That relationship is permanently secure if you've accepted Christ. In the same way you cannot decide to be unborn from your physical, or first birth, you cannot determine to become unborn once you have experienced your spiritual, second birth.

"SAVED…THROUGH FIRE"

It sounds odd to use the phrase "getting into heaven" in the same sentence with words like "sadly" and "unfortunately." Yet, tragically, some will make it, as the old expression goes, "by the skin of their teeth." They've received the Lord, but lived such unproductive Christian lives that they'll have little to show for it at the judgment. As the Bible says, they'll *"Be saved, yet so as through fire"* (1 Corinthians 3:15).

If you still struggle with the idea that regret, in any form, could seep into the jubilation of heaven, consider the following scenario. My insurance agent calls and says my homeowner's policy has lapsed and I'm not covered. I assure him I'll take care of the situation but I don't. Two weeks later, a tornado rips through my neighborhood and levels our house. My family escapes bodily injury, yet we lose nearly everything we own.

Rummaging through the rubble the next day, emotions swirl through my mind. I'm thrilled that my wife and children are safe. Stuff can be replaced, people can't. But, at the same time, I am regretful that I failed to make proper preparation—especially after being warned.

Just like we were saved from the storm and still suffered loss, millions will escape the "flames of judgment," yet rue the missed possibilities. These missed opportunities include **rewards** that will constitute a key element of judgment seat activity.

This truth creates a spiritual paradox. Our driving motive in kingdom life should be to please God and serve others. However, Scripture teaches that believers can anticipate the following tributes, the first being *praise*. If you appreciate being told that you're doing a good job and making a difference, just think what it's going to be like hearing it from Christ.

"WELL DONE"

Just days before being crucified, Jesus told a parable that contains specific end time implications. Before leaving on a journey, a master gave three of his servants money—five, two and one talents respectively. While the boss was away, one servant buried his talent. The other two, however, doubled their money. The master returned and said to these two, *"Well done, good and faithful slave. You were faithful with a few things, I will put you in charge of many things. Enter into the joy of your master"* (Matthew 25:21,23).

Because the servant was faithful with a little, he was given authority over a lot. This clearly indicates the possibility in eternity for *increased responsibility*. Perhaps you're thinking, "I want less responsibility, not more. I figured heaven would be one big "kick back and relax" experience. After all, I'm tired."

I know how you feel. I'm tired too. But remember, we're tired because of the sinful conditions in which we live. Work became tedious and tiresome *after* the Fall. In the new creation, with the curse removed, Eden-like conditions will prevail. "We will enjoy the responsibility God gives us, but the degree of fulfillment we experience will depend upon our faithfulness to Christ in this life."[3]

I'm expecting some surprises. Even if they escape the second death, many wielding great power and authority in this world won't do so in the world to come. Yet, those who transform an insignificant social standing, limited education, meager resources and minimal opportunity into prosperous kingdom living on this earth can expect a significant promotion on the earth to come.

Afterlife rewards in the Bible also includes *crowns*. The five mentioned specifically in the New Testament are:

The Incorruptible Crown—Paul said that athletes go into strict training to get *"a crown that will not last; but we do it for a crown that will last forever"* (1 Corinthians 9:25, NIV). Paul was referring to the celery and laurel crowns given to athletic winners in the first century, which would wilt within days of being received. However, believers who qualify for the victor's crown on judgment day will receive crowns that last forever.

Crown of Rejoicing—Also called the soul winner's crown, Paul describes this prize as well. *"For who is our hope or joy or crown of exultation? Is it not even you, in the presence of our Lord Jesus at His coming?"* (1 Thessalonians 2:19). The Apostle refers here to members of the church at Thessalonica that became believers because of his missionary work. What could be more invigorating than seeing someone in heaven that you've led to the Lord?

Crown of Righteousness—Again, Paul details the reward, this time to Timothy. *"In the future there is laid up for me the crown of righteousness, which the Lord, the righteous Judge, will award to me on that day; and not only to me, but also to all who have loved His appearing"* (2 Timothy 4:8). The Apostle wasn't afraid to express his confident expectation of receiving this award. There's no reason that Christians who diligently serve the Lord and desire His spiritual and physical presence can't exude that same bold expectation.

Crown of Glory—Here, Peter addresses elders in the church. *"Shepherd the flock of God among you . . . not under compulsion, but voluntarily . . . not for sordid gain, but with eagerness . . . And when the Chief Shepherd appears, you will receive the unfading crown of glory"* (1 Peter 5:2-4). Although church leaders should never consider themselves above those whom they serve, here they are promised a special privilege related to Jesus' return and God's glory. And like the Incorruptible Crown described above, this prize will maintain its spiritual luster throughout eternity.

Crown of Life—Two New Testament authors write about this reward. James said, *"Blessed is the man who perseveres under trial, because once he has been approved, he will receive the crown of life which the Lord has promised to those who love Him"* (James 1:12). Jesus told those intensely persecuted at Smyrna, *"Be faithful unto death, and I will give you the crown of life"* (Revelation 2:10). This crown is synonymous with eternal life. Sin, sickness, suffering, etc. take away our temporal, earthly existence; but nothing can jeopardize the forever, fulfilling life that awaits those belonging to Christ. And though specific reference is made to sufferers, this crown awaits all believers.

Some people get a little uncomfortable with a discussion about the rewards of heaven because the focus is on man rather than Christ. But understand, the purpose of these rewards is not for us to parade up and down the golden streets, drawing attention to our accomplishments. Also, I can't see us displaying crowns on the mantle like trophies. More than likely, we'll imitate the twenty-four elders mentioned in John's vision and place any crowns we have received before the throne of God (Revelation 4:10).

Finally, rewards for the believer come in the form of *special privileges.* The Bible says that if we enhance our faith with increasing *"Moral excellence, knowledge, self-control, perseverance, godliness, brotherly kindness and love"* we can expect an *"abundantly supplied"* entrance into the Lord's kingdom (2 Peter 1:5-11)—as opposed to barely making it in.

In addition to this red-carpet greeting, Jesus told of another added honor for those particularly honed in on His plan: *"Blessed are those slaves whom the master will find on the alert when he comes . . . he will gird himself to serve, and will come and wait on them"* (Luke 12:37).

There are believers among us who, though prepared, are not watching for his coming. Many of those are part of the "wood, hay and straw" mass previously mentioned—those who enter heaven by narrowly escaping the flames (see 1 Corinthians 3:15). Thankfully, millions of faithful have lived and are living that can anticipate having their Chief Shepherd wait on them.

During a *Primetime Live* interview, Billy Graham was asked, "What do you want people to say about you when you're gone?" He responded: "I don't want them to say anything about me. I want them to talk about my Savior. The only thing I want to hear is Jesus saying, 'Well done, My good and faithful servant.' *But I'm not sure I'm going to hear that."*[4]

It's not my place to judge, but I'm certain Dr. Graham will indeed hear that. I hope that you and I do too.

17

THE SECOND DEATH

"If anyone's name was not found written in the book of life, he was thrown into the lake of fire" (Revelation 20:15).

ಬಿಂಚಿ

Two preachers stood together by the side of the road between their churches, feverishly hammering a handmade sign into the ground that read:

**THE END IS NEAR
TURN AROUND NOW
BEFORE IT'S TOO LATE!**

Suddenly, a car sped past them with the driver yelling out the window, "Leave us alone, you religious fanatics!"

After hearing the screeching of tires and a big splash, one turned to the other and said, "Do you think the sign should have simply said **BRIDGE OUT AHEAD** instead?"

By nature, people, especially those running from God, are turned off by the subject of religious fervor as it relates to hell. And yet, as discovered in chapter 13, the Bible speaks clearly and extensively on the subject.

I've had people say, "We're all after the same goal, headed for the same place, so, what's the big deal?" The big deal is that we most assuredly are not all going to the same place. If you've been born again, saved, received Christ into your heart, or whatever terminology you want to use to indicate you are a child of God, you can look forward to going to heaven when you die as we recently discussed. If you haven't experienced the above, Scripture emphatically says that you'll spend eternity in hell.

In chapter 13, we dealt primarily with *Hades*, the place of temporary anguish and misery that imprisons unbelievers until the end times. Recall the unnamed rich man who enjoyed lavish prosperity on earth, only to endure great torment following his death. He found himself in a state of separation from God and permanent hopelessness. Now let's switch emphasis from the first death to the second death, from *Hades* to *Gehenna* —with the main thrust being on the condemnation that comes before the destination.

Exiled on Patmos, John "*Saw a great white throne and Him who sat upon it*" (Revelation 20:11). Certainly, it's God who sits upon the throne, as is usually the case in Revelation. The color white indicates His purity, glory, majesty and qualification for carrying out this somber, but necessary task.

The great white throne judgment is preceded by the **permanent banishment of the devil.** Remember from chapter 13 that when Christ returns, Satan is bound for a thousand years. After that time of banishment, he's released and allowed to deceive one final time. Then, according to John's vision, he will be "*Thrown into the lake of fire and brimstone, where the beast and the false prophet are also*" (Revelation 20:10).

RISING TO CONDEMNATION

Originally, hell was not a place planned for humans. Speaking to the unfaithful servants, or the goats, Jesus said, *"Depart from Me, accursed ones, into the eternal fire which has been prepared for the devil and his angels"* (Matthew 25:41). Tragically, men and women who follow Satan in rebellion must share in this destination.

This final judgment also involves **a second resurrection.** According to Jesus: *"An hour is coming, in which all who are in the tombs will hear His voice, and will come forth; those who did the good deeds to a resurrection of life, those who committed evil deeds to a resurrection of judgment"* (John 5:28,29). It comes as no surprise that those doing good will rise to live. We discussed this previously when speaking of the Second Coming.

What seems a little unusual, yet it's absolutely biblical, is the rising of the dead unbelievers, those having done evil. After speaking of a pre-millennial resurrection of saints, John says, *"The rest of the dead (unbelievers) did not come to life until the thousand years were completed,"* adding later, *"The sea gave up the dead which were in it, and death and Hades gave up the dead which were in them"* (Revelation 20:5,13). This confirms the claim that Hades is not the final fate for those who've rejected Christ. Otherwise, why would Hades "give up" residents if that was their permanent destination?

Observe, too, that those appearing at the great white throne **are judged by what they have done** (Revelation 20:12,13). Please understand that this isn't suggesting a salvation based on good works. The Bible clearly states that we are saved by grace, not by works (Ephesians 2:8,9). Also, this doesn't mean that one's eternal destiny hangs in the balance at this point. Salvation is determined in life, not at death.

Those subjected to this punishment are being judged according to their works because they have failed to appropriate the work Christ carried out on the Cross on their behalf. The works of believers at the judgment seat carry significant weight because our salvation is already secure. As previously stated, works there determine reception of loss or reward.

Hypothetically, let's say an unbeliever put together a five-minute multi-media presentation of the most religious and righteous moments of his/her life to present to the Lord on judgment day. Contained in this presentation is the person feeding the hungry, attending church regularly, giving generously and serving those in need. Having viewed the tape, Jesus tosses it aside and says, *"Away from Me, I never knew you."* Why the rejection? It's because the person relied solely on their own performance to get them into heaven. That's the way it will be for those who are judged during the great white throne judgment. They're rejected because their works fail to meet the rigorous standards of Christ. Isaiah said, *"All our righteous deeds are like a filthy garment"* (Isaiah 64:6)—a spiritual truth which is nowhere more applicable than for the lost person on judgment day.

John writes that our works are recorded in **books**: *"And books were opened; and another book was opened, which is the book of life; and the dead were judged from the things written in the books, according to their deeds . . . If anyone's name was not found written in the book of life..."* (Revelation 20:12,15).

This is one of the numerous times that salvation is equated with books and writing. When the disciples returned excitedly from a mission venture, Jesus said, *"Do not rejoice in this; that the spirits are subject to you, but rejoice that your names are recorded in heaven"* (Luke 10:20). Paul sought help for colleagues whose names *"Are in the book of life"* (Philippians 4:3). John even terms it the "Lamb's book of life" later in Revelation (Revelation 21:27).

Tragically, those brought before the great white throne are those whose names do not appear in this book of life. As stated, good deeds that have been recorded in one book are not sufficient to get one's name written in the other.

HAVE YOU RSVP'D?

I heard a story recently about a singer named Ruth Metzger, who was called upon to sing at the wedding of a very wealthy man. The invitation stated that the reception would take place on the top two floors of Seattle's Columbia Tower, the tallest building in Northwest America.

At the reception, tuxedoed waiters served delicious hors d'oeuvres and exotic drinks. As the bride and groom made their way to a breathtaking glass and brass staircase that led to the top floor, someone cut a satin ribbon that hung across the bottom of the stairs. The couple began their ascent, followed by the guests, as the feast was formally announced. At the top, a maitre d' with book in hand welcomed guests outside the doors.

"May I have your name please?"

"I am Ruthanna Metzger and this is my husband, Roy."

He scanned the *M*'s. "I'm not finding it. Would you spell it please?"

Ruth spelled it out carefully. Sadly, after searching his list again, the gentleman said, "I'm sorry, but your name isn't here."

"There must be some mistake," Ruth replied. "I'm the singer. I sang for this wedding!"

"It doesn't matter who you are or what you did" the maitre d' replied. "Without your name in the book you cannot attend the banquet." He called to a waiter, "Show these people to the service elevator, please."

The waiter walked the Metzger's past tables of shrimp, whole smoked salmon, ice sculptures, etc. He then let them into the elevator and pushed G for parking garage. After the couple located their car and drove in despair several miles down the road, Roy said to his wife, "Sweetheart, what happened?"

"When the invitation arrived, I was busy," she answered. "I never bothered to RSVP. Besides, I was the singer. Surely I could go to the reception without returning the RSVP."

Ruthanna started to weep—not only because she had missed the most lavish banquet she'd ever been invited to, but also because she suddenly had a small taste of what it will be like someday for people as they stand before Christ and find their names are not written in the Lamb's Book of Life.[1]

That "someday" will come at the great white throne judgment. But instead of returning to a normal life by way of a service elevator, those present will experience the second death by being **thrown into the lake of fire.**

Since I dealt with this issue in the chapter on hell, I won't spend much time with it here. And though I believe the rich man/Lazarus parable deals specifically with *Hades, Gehenna* is certainly described as being fiery too. Jesus said in a verse I touched on earlier, *"It is better for you to enter life crippled, than, having your two hands, to go into hell (Gehenna), into the unquenchable fire"* (Mark 9:43,44).

The issue is eternal affliction versus annihilation. What lost person wouldn't welcome the idea of a quick torching at the judgment, with no accountability to follow? Yet the Bible teaches that the pain and agony doesn't end at the great white throne, but goes on forever and ever (Revelation 20:10).

A CONSUMING FIRE

See finally, this judgment provides the backdrop for **a complete destruction of the heavens and the earth**. As creation was included in the fall, so it will be included in the judgment as well. The pounding the earth endures during the great tribulation, after which Jesus comes to provide restoration, is but a foretaste of the greater destruction that comes during this final judgment. This time, it takes more than a beating. The Bible says, *"The day of the Lord will come like a thief, in which the heavens will pass away with a roar and the elements will be destroyed with intense heat, and the earth and its works will be burned up"* (2 Peter 3:10).

Ponder this verse and see first that the sky will vanish with a "roar." The term used for roar "is a colorful . . .word which can be used of the swish of an arrow through the air, or the rumbling of thunder, as well as the crackling of flames, the scream of the lash as it descends, the rushing of mighty waters, or the hissing of a serpent."[2]

Fire enters the picture once again by destroying the elements and burning up the earth, along with everything in it. Although the word "elements" is a bit confusing, it undoubtedly refers to the materials that make up the earth. There's no doubt about the fact that this present planet and its structures will be completely obliterated. This is consistent with the close connection between God, fire and judgment. As Moses commanded the children of Israel before they entered Canaan, *"So watch yourselves, that you do not forget the covenant of the LORD your God . . . For the LORD your God is a consuming fire . . ."* (Deuteronomy 4:23, 24)—a warning the writer of Hebrews borrowed when writing about the danger of refusing God (Hebrews 12:29).

Peter's writing also jibes with what John observed: *"Earth and heaven fled away, and no place was for them. The first heaven and the first earth passed away, and there is no longer any sea"* (Revelation 20:11, 21:1).

"Checkmate" is an old painting portraying the so-called triumph of the devil in a chess game. He is shown celebrating the apparent failure of his opponent. All indications are that the young man seated at the chessboard has lost. His expression exudes hopelessness and dejection.

Fascinated by the painting, a famous chess player sought to see if there was any way the young man could win. He placed the pieces on his board exactly as they appeared on the canvas and studied them carefully. All at once, he jumped to his feet and exclaimed, "The painting is wrong! There is a way out!"

Unfortunately, for those at the great white throne, that will not be the case. Yet, there's still time for those without Christ who still live on this earth. If you're part of that group, I pray that you receive the new life that eliminates the second death.

18

PARADISE RESTORED

"Then I saw a new heaven and a new earth"
(Revelation 21:1).

৪৩৫৪

An avid golfer selected his club and stepped anxiously onto the tee of a par three. Since the hole required a shot over water, he pulled an old, scarred, discolored ball out of his bag and prepared to hit it.

Suddenly, a voice from heaven said, "use a new ball." Dumbfounded, the guy asked his buddies if they heard a voice. When they said no, he stood over his old ball a second time. Once again, a voice rang out, "use a new ball."

Reluctantly, the golfer went to his bag and pulled out a brand-new ball of the highest quality—the kind the professionals use. And then, for a third time, the words rang out, "take a practice swing." Immediately, the man reached back and followed through, digging out a huge hunk of turf in the process.

He then received these final instructions: "use an old ball."

Todd Gaddis

A day is coming when God will transform this "old ball" on which we live into a "new ball." In fact, a new heaven will come with the deal.

The last chapter concluded with the complete destruction by fire of the heavens and earth as they now exist. The Bible says a restored paradise will follow on the heels of this catastrophic event. During his Patmos visions, John *"saw a new heaven and a new earth, for the first heaven and the first earth had passed away, and there was no longer any sea"* (Revelation 21:1).

Note the new earth will consist of a new **city**, known first for its *beauty* —like a woman dressed up for her husband on their wedding day. I've done numerous weddings in my sixteen years as a pastor and the brides always sparkle with a special glow. My wife never looked prettier than that summer day in 1983 when she walked down the aisle and took my arm. Likewise, Jerusalem will shine like never before.

John caught a sneak preview of this truth by witnessing a place of *"brilliance . . . like that of a very precious jewel, like a jasper, clear as crystal"* (Revelation 21:11). The new Jerusalem will be made of pure gold. Walls around the city will be decorated with various kinds of precious stones. Gates along the walls will be made of pearl. Currently, such costly valuables sit in safes, glass cases and tightly guarded museums. In the world to come, they'll be out in the open, for everyone to see and enjoy.

The new Jerusalem will also be known for its *immensity*. When John saw the city, he measured it to be 1,400 miles in width, length and height (Revelation 21:16). "A metropolis of this size in the middle of the United States would stretch from Canada to Mexico and from the Appalachian Mountains to the California border."[1] If the city is made up of multiple levels, with each floor being twelve feet high, it will contain over 600,000 stories! Believers who have suffered in crowded quarters on this old, fallen earth can look forward to plenty of elbowroom on the new earth.

Finally, the Holy City will be a place of unprecedented *purity*. God told John, "*Nothing impure will ever enter it, nor will anyone who does what is shameful or deceitful*" (Revelation 21:27). Cities across our globe suffer the blight of moral decadence. Such will not be the case in the age to come.

The Word also tells us that the entrance to the city will never be closed (Revelation 21:26). In ancient times, the gates of walled cities were secured at night to guard against enemy attack. I carefully lock and deadbolt our doors at night, and often during the day, to guard against possible intruders. Thankfully, this won't be necessary when God establishes His Kingdom exclusively on this earth.

This purity and security is a byproduct of a total **peace** that will engulf not only the Jerusalem to come, but the new heaven and new earth in their entirety. Currently, we can enjoy peace *with* God (Romans 5:1) and the peace *of* God (Philippians 4:7). Yet, a *future* peace that eludes us in this present age still awaits.

I believe this end of time peace has sociological, biological, and geological ramifications. Rarely a week goes by without some mention of a truce between the Arabs and the Israelis, peace between warring factions in Africa and the Middle East, etc. I'm thrilled at such prospects, yet nothing permanent is going to happen until the Prince of Peace comes to establish His reign on earth.

I read recently about a snake and rodent that became best friends at a Tokyo zoo. Gohan, the 3.5-inch dwarf hamster, was served to a four-foot rat snake named Aochan for dinner. Instead of becoming a meal for the snake, however, Gohan became its friend. "I've never seen anything like it. Gohan sometimes even climbs onto Aochan to take a nap on his back. Aochan seems to enjoy Gohan's company very much," said zookeeper Kazuya Yamamoto.[2]

Although this makes a great human-interest story, it's an aberration. Typically, the snake would devour the rodent. It's the law of the old earth jungle. However, a time is coming when the rules will change. On the future earth: "*The wolf will live with the lamb, the leopard will lie down with the goat, the calf and the lion and the yearling together, and the lion will eat straw like the ox. The infant will play near the hole of the cobra, and the young child put his hand into the viper's nest"* (Isaiah 11:7,8).

WHEN MAN FELL, CREATION FELL

Paul says, *"creation waits in eager expectation for the sons of God to be revealed."* It *"has been groaning as in the pains of childbirth right up to the present time"* (Romans 8:19,22). When mankind fell, creation fell. Sin blighted the physical earth as well as the souls of humans. Creation grows increasingly weary of decay and disaster. It longs for a time void of hurricanes, tornadoes, earthquakes, volcanic eruptions, tsunamis, etc. The new heaven and new earth peace will usher in such an era.

Another key element of the new earth is the presence of a **river** —*"the river of the water of life, as clear as crystal, flowing from the throne of God and of the Lamb down the middle of the great street of the city"* (Revelation 22:1,2).

Some see this merely as a symbol of God's presence, but I beg to differ. Just like literal rivers (Pishon, Gihon, Tigris and Euphrates) held prominence in Paradise before the fall, I view this as an actual river with great visibility on the new earth.

Note, first its *source*. Every river starts somewhere. I grew up on the banks of the mighty Ohio in western Kentucky. This 981-mile waterway originates at the confluence of the Allegheny and Monongahela rivers in downtown Pittsburg. The world's longest river, Africa's 4,160-mile Nile, has Lake Victoria as its source.

No river on the old earth, however, can compare to this body of water on the earth to come, which originates at the throne and Lamb of God. This clearly indicates that God is the source of all life. God said, *"whoever finds me finds life"* (Proverbs 8:35). Jesus proclaimed, *"I am the . . . life"* (John 14:6). These truths will be evident in the age to come.

Next, follow the river's *course*. The Bible says it *flows **down the middle** of the great street of the city* (Revelation 22:2, emphasis added). This geographic placement suggests prominence and enables access.

John provides evidence of this by describing the river's bountiful *harvest*. First, there's the tree of life, which will yield a crop of fruit every month. Remember from chapter one that this tree was originally designed to provide nourishment to Adam and Eve. After the fall, however, it became off limits. That will all change in the new Paradise. God's children from throughout the ages, joined by Adam and Eve, will be able to enjoy this tasty, perpetual fruit.

God's Word tells us that the leaves of this tree serve to heal the nations. A skeptic might wonder why healing would be necessary in a perfectly healthy environment. "The healing leaves indicate the complete absence of physical and spiritual want. The life to come will be a life of abundance and perfection."[3]

Some of you may be thinking, "that's all well and good, but I'd like to tap into some of that abundance right now"—to which I say "Amen." Jesus came that we might have abundant life (John 10:10). He promised that, *"He that believeth on me, as the scripture hath said, out of his belly shall flow rivers of living water"* (John 7:38, KJV). In a sense, Christians become God's kingdom on this earth, instruments through which the Holy Spirit can pour forth His blessings.

But as exciting, available and prominent as the river, peace and city are, they all pale in comparison to the future **literal presence** of God among His children. With the coming of the Holy City, *"the dwelling of God is with men, and he will live with them. They will be his people, and God himself will be with them and be their God"* (Revelation 21:3).

Throughout redemptive history, God's presence has been manifested in various ways. "In the Old Testament it was mediated through the prophetic word, theophanies, dreams, angels and the cult. To come face to face with the living God meant death" (Exodus 33:20).[4] God became one of us when Jesus appeared the first time

2000 years ago. Since He died, rose and ascended to His original home, the Holy Spirit has represented the Trinity on earth (John 16:7). As detailed in chapter 15, Christ will return at the end of the great tribulation. And then, God Himself will come to live among us at the conclusion of the millennium and culmination of the end times. Gloriously and finally, we shall see His face (Revelation 22:4).

Being with God up close and personal will facilitate worship like none we've ever experienced. Old earth worship is often too categorized, scrutinized and individualized—emphasizing style at the expense of substance. Yet, the unprecedented, untainted praise I described in chapter 14 will carry over from heaven to the new earth.

ADORATION WITHOUT ABSORPTION

I've had men in my church return from stadium ministry events raving about the chill bumps they get when tens of thousands join in song. Just think what it's going to be like in a choir in the millions, with the Holy Trinity personally present –and angels joining in.

Please don't confuse this endless adoration with total absorption. I've seen moms and dads so absorbed in their children that nothing else seems to matter. People become so devoured by their jobs that everything else falls apart. And while it's true that we, along with the rest of the saints and angels, will be worshipping God forever and ever, that's not *all* we'll be doing.

For example, the new earth will include such normal activities as *eating, drinking and resting*. Remember, this chapter's central text tells of feeding from the tree of life. The fact that end times are associated with a great wedding feast tells me that many other delicacies await. If you doubt that our glorified bodies will require food, recall that the risen Jesus ate breakfast with His disciples along the shore of the Sea of Galilee (John 21:12).

One of my favorite verses to use at funerals says, *"Blessed are the dead who die in the Lord from now on. Yes," says the Spirit "they will **rest** from their labor . . ."* (Revelation 14:13, emphasis added). I believe this rest will include sleep. Presumably, Adam and Eve slept before the fall. There's no reason to doubt that it will be enjoyed on the new earth.

A skeptic might ask, "Why should we sleep when we won't get fatigued from working?" On the contrary, I believe we will grow tired because we will be ***working***—it just won't seem like the cursed, old world labor just mentioned. Adam and Eve "worked" in Eden prior to the fall (Genesis 2:15). In the parable of the talents, the faithful who doubled their money were promised more responsibility in the afterlife (Matthew 25:21,23). Obviously, responsibility implies service and service implies work. Scripture says that servants of the Lamb will serve Him on the new earth (Revelation 22:3).

Finally, I contend that our world to come will include ***fellowshipping, traveling and learning—enjoying every aspect of the new heavens and earth.***

In addition to our adoration of God, we will enjoy fellowship with our fellow believers. There won't be wedlock in heaven (Matthew 22:30), because holy matrimony is an old earth institution superseded by the marriage of the Church and the Lamb. Having said that, I still believe we'll enjoy stronger relationships with spouses, children, parents, siblings and other extended family. Although it sounds confusing and contradictory, it's a mystery that will be cleared up in the world to come. Whatever the case, don't fret about it. "God usually doesn't replace his original creation, but when he does, he replaces it with something that is far better, never worse."[5]

This perfect fellowship will extend beyond families and into friendships. We'll become even closer to friends in the life to come that we've made in this one. And to think, this will happen in the absence of jealousy, cliques, conflict, etc.

Todd Gaddis

Will animals be present? Why not? If they existed before the fall, they'll be there in the new paradise. This doesn't mean we'll be reunited with pets that have died. However, I do believe we'll enjoy God's creatures in a transformed atmosphere of safety and playfulness.

In the resurrected world, we will also find pleasure and gratification in the inanimate side of creation. With so many beautiful places to see on this doomed planet, just imagine what's in store when the curse is removed. Many are kept from personally enjoying such sights now because of lack of finances, career responsibilities, etc. These and other restrictions won't exist in the world to come.

Notice that I include the heavens too. Since we've gone to the moon under sin's dominion, imagine the new galaxies we'll explore in the world to come. "What will we be able to accomplish for God's glory when we have resurrected minds, unlimited resources, complete scientific cooperation, and no more death?"[6]

In other words, learning won't cease with the destruction of the old earth. Rather, it will take on all new dimensions. Puritan theologian Jonathan Edwards said, "The saints will be progressive in knowledge to all eternity."[7] The height of this fresh comprehension will center upon God's Word, since the Bible says it will remain forever (Psalm 119:89, Matthew 24:35).

In 1952, Florence Chadwick entered Pacific Ocean waters off Catalina Island, determined to swim to the shore of mainland California. She was already the first woman to swim the English Channel in both directions. In cold, foggy conditions, she could barely see the boats alongside her. Resolute, she continued for fifteen hours.

When she pleaded to be taken out of the water, her mother in a nearby boat told her she was close and urged her on. Emotionally and physically drained, Frances eventually got pulled from the water, only to discover that she was less than half a mile from her destination. "All I could see was the fog . . . I think if I could have seen the shore, I would have made it."

Despite coming up short, she attempted the same feat two months later. This time she completed the 26-mile swim—the first woman to do so—shaving two hours off the men's record. The same fog loomed again, yet she succeeded on this occasion by maintaining a mental image of the shoreline in her mind, thus achieving her goal.[1]

As you face the frequent battles and occasional boredom of everyday life, "*Set your mind on the things above, not on the things that are on earth*" (Colossians 3:2). Appropriate Scripture and visualize the permanent paradise that awaits.

Todd Gaddis

19

THE GREAT COMMANDMENT

"Love the Lord your God . . ."
(Matthew 22:37).

&)&

It would have made perfect sense to end our journey with believers living happily ever after on the New Earth. I've baked the cake, assembled the layers, iced, and decorated it. Yet one thing is missing, an inscription on top. I'll do that now: **Love.**

As Jesus was preaching and teaching one day, He conversed with a lawyer (Luke 10:25-29). The Bible says the man *"stood up and put Him to the test"* (Luke10:25). In place of the word "test," the KJV uses "tempted," which implies this legal expert was feigning interest, yet attempting to get the Lord to contradict the written law. Perhaps he was looking for an opportunity to display his knowledge and show Jesus up. Whatever the motivation, this dialogue created an excellent instructional opportunity.

The curious lawyer began with the first of two questions: *"What shall I do to inherit eternal life?"*(Luke 10:25). Always the consummate teacher, the Lord answered the question with a question, *"What is written in the Law? How does it read to you?"*(Luke 10:26). The man responded with the following commands from Deuteronomy and Leviticus: *"YOU SHALL LOVE THE LORD YOUR GOD WITH ALL YOUR HEART, AND WITH ALL YOUR STRENGTH, AND WITH ALL YOUR MIND; AND YOUR NEIGHBOR AS YOURSELF"* (Luke 10:27).

Jesus affirmed the lawyer's answer, which may sound surprising, since it seems to suggest salvation by works. Yet, nothing could be further from the truth. "Jesus is not commending a new system of legalism somewhat different from the old, but pointing to the end of all legalism."[1] The lawyer wanted to gain access to heaven by keeping a set of regulations. The Lord turns this system upside down by telling him that eternal life is not a matter of rules but rather of love.

Because God is love, He's the obvious source of all true love. The ultimate demonstration of such love came when He sent His only Son Jesus to die for our sins. The "greatest commandment," as one Gospel writer put it, compels us to reciprocate.

Note carefully that the first portion of Jesus' challenge emphasizes the importance of the **vertical connection between people and God**. We'll never have right relationships with others if we don't first establish one with God. Loving people begins with loving God.

A farmer visiting London for the first time wandered into an art gallery. Seeing a painting of Jesus on the Cross, he stood transfixed. Oblivious to those around him, he cried out, "Bless the Lord! Oh how I love Him, how I love Him." As people began to take notice, a stranger walked up and said, "I love Him too." Then another grabbed his hand and tremblingly spoke, "And I love Him too." A third came, then a fourth, and still another until before long a band of bold believers stood together before the artwork—strangers brought together in Christ, prompted by a simple man who wasn't afraid to express his love.[2]

HOW ARE YOU DOING?

Jesus affirmed that we are to love with our "heart, soul, strength, and mind"—this clearly indicates that we are to love broadly and deeply— with every bit of who we are. Unfortunately, we too often mimic the pattern of Old Testament Jews by drawing near to God with our lips while our hearts remain far away (Isaiah 29:13). Rather than getting bogged down in rules taught by men, we must immerse ourselves in a love relationship with the Lord.

Imagine pouring water from a pitcher into a glass that sits on a countertop. If you keep pouring after the glass is full, water will overflow and spread sideways. Likewise, as you continue to grow in your *vertical* relationship with God, such adoration and affection should supernaturally spill out, spreading **horizontally to those around you.** That enables us to demonstrate part two of this great commandment, loving our neighbor as ourselves.

Notice that we are not commanded to love our neighbor *instead* of ourselves. Just because we are instructed to consider others better than ourselves (Philippians 2:3) doesn't mean that we aren't to love ourselves. In fact, those who struggle to love themselves have trouble loving others as well. And once the lawyer reiterated what was written in the law, Jesus replied, *"DO THIS AND YOU WILL LIVE"* (Luke 10:28).

The expert would not let the matter rest. The Bible says *"He wanted to justify himself"* (Luke 10:29, NIV). Was he trying to limit the scope of the law and thus his own responsibility? Whatever the case, this paved the way for his second question: *"And who is my neighbor?"* (Luke 10:29).

The Lord enriched the conversation, answering the question with His favorite teaching tool, the parable. This particular account tells of a man who was beaten, robbed and left to die on the road between Jerusalem and Jericho (read Luke 10:30-37). After a priest and Levite passed by without helping the man, a Samaritan stopped to help the wounded traveler. Carefully consider these lessons on love that surface from this parable.

Show that you care. When the Samaritan saw the wounded man, *"He felt compassion"* (Luke 10:33). The word used in the original language implies a deep feeling of sympathy. It's the same verb Jesus used after looking over a hungry crowd of thousands. *"I feel compassion for the people because they have remained with Me now three days and have nothing to eat."* (Mark 8:2).

Mother Teresa is an icon of sympathy and service. On one occasion she was brought face to face with a man who had a rare and horrendous case of terminal cancer. One of the workers had vomited from the stench and could no longer continue. Mother Teresa then stepped in and kindly took over. The patient was mystified. "How can you stand the smell?" asked the patient. Mother Teresa replied, "It's nothing compared to the pain you must feel."[3]

"PERFECT LOVE DRIVES OUT FEAR"

The Good Samaritan demonstrated that same compassion. Grasping the severity of the situation, he began tending the victim's injuries. He used wine to cleanse the wounds and oil to ease the pain—but he didn't stop there.

Had the beaten and robbed man been left to fend for himself along the side of the road, he might have been the victim of more misfortune. Other degenerates might have come along. Dangerous animals could have attacked. Therefore, the Samaritan put the man on his donkey and took him to an inn to provide a place for refuge and healing.

It may sound trite, but it's absolutely true: "People don't care what you know till they know that you care." Put your religion into action by exhibiting Christ-like tenderness. Love demands evidence of care and concern—and that isn't all. You must also:

Step outside of your box, which may require *overcoming fear.* The Good Samaritan certainly did. How could he be sure this crime was not staged? What if the victim was actually part of a band of robbers—with the rest of the gang lurking in the shadows, waiting to take advantage of the first person to stop.

I'm not suggesting you make unwise or irresponsible decisions and put your life at risk. Stopping for strangers could lead to disaster. However, if you follow the lead of the Holy Spirit, He will guide and protect in such situations.

Certainly, many other less daring needs and opportunities exist. For example, are there positions or projects where you could plug in? Could you volunteer at an area food mission or homeless shelter? Would you consider going on a short term mission trip? Have you shared the plan of salvation with someone and led them to faith in Jesus Christ?

These suggestions may create a sense of fear in you, but they shouldn't. The Bible says, *"For God hath not given us the spirit of fear; but of power, and of love, and of a sound mind"* (2 Timothy 1:7, KJV). *"Perfect love casts out fear"* (1 John 4:18).

Don't be afraid to move beyond the comfortable. Consider the possibility that God has a wonderful blessing in store if only you'll conquer your fears, branch away from the well-worn paths, and venture into uncharted territory.

Stepping outside of your box often means *putting aside your prejudices* as well. Since Jews often referred to Samaritans as "half-breeds" and "dogs," this lawyer must surely have been taken aback by the fact that this man was the only one among the three to stop and offer assistance.

Mahatma Gandhi wrote in his autobiography that during his student days he read the Gospels and seriously considered converting to Christianity. He believed the teachings of Jesus could provide the solution to the caste system that divided the people of India.

Therefore, he decided to attend a nearby church and talk to the minister about becoming a Christian. However, when Gandhi entered the sanctuary, an usher refused to seat him and suggested that he go and worship with his own people.

"If Christians have caste systems also," he said, "I might as well remain a Hindu." The usher's prejudice betrayed Jesus and also turned a person away from trusting Him as Savior.[4]

Of course, our prejudices are certainly not limited to race. I live in the South where people sometimes don't accept "Yankees" from the North. I've lived in the North and witnessed stereotypes against Southerners as well.

The prosperous often look down upon the poor. Even though the church I pastor has members from all walks of life, we've been labeled in the past as coming from the upper class and social elite. (I'm happy to report this is changing for the good). Likewise, the educated often look with disdain upon the uneducated, and vice versa. Such biases must be set aside if we're to live as Jesus lived.

LOVE IS SPELLED T-I-M-E

Being a good neighbor also requires a willingness to *give of your resources.* And though I dealt with this vital subject in Chapter 11, let's give it one more push as we again examine the following two challenges:

Show love by giving/sharing time—The Good Samaritan certainly did. Obviously, he had somewhere to be. Yet that didn't keep him from stopping to help someone in need. He increased his time commitment substantially by taking the victim to an inn and agreeing to come back later to settle.

You've probably heard about the boy that was asked how to spell love. "We spell it T.I.M.E. at our house." the lad responded. Time is more valuable than money to many in this 21st Century economy in which we live.

As He went about preaching, teaching, and healing, Jesus valued the individual, often spending time with them. He asked the women at the well for a drink and then spent the necessary time to tell her about living water. (John 4). Later, with the crucifixion just days away, He stopped to visit with a Jewish tax collector. The two then went to Zacchaeus' house where they continued the conversation (Luke 19:1-10). In both cases, those who Jesus spent time with repented of their sins and received salvation.

Show love by giving your money—As God's hold on us tightens, we begin to view money from an eternal perspective—God is the owner and we are the stewards. We become bolder, less selfish, and more generous in our stewardship.

Such was the case with the Good Samaritan. He not only covered the immediate expenses of the victim, but additional costs when he returned.

You can give without loving but you can't love without giving. Be open to fresh, new ways to share your resources.

Focus on this challenge as we conclude this section on spreading the love horizontally: *"Above all, keep fervent in your love for one another, because* **love covers a multitude of sins"** (1 Peter 4:8, emphasis added). It is interesting to note that the Greek word for fervent, *ektenes,* suggests athletes stretching and straining muscles in an exerted effort. This is not a warm and fuzzy love that God calls us to, but one of strenuous intention.

If I could condense these faith essentials into one word, it would be "love." Love takes precedent over all other fruits, virtues, and characteristics. Giving people the benefit of the doubt, we ought to make every effort to maintain love in a relationship, no matter what has happened or how difficult the situation becomes. As Paul writes, *"Now faith, hope, love, abide these three; but the greatest of these is love"* (1 Corinthians 13:13).

Allen Emery, a dear friend of Billy Graham's, had an experience as a young boy which made a deep impression upon him. His father received a call saying a well-known Christian had been found at a certain place drunk on the sidewalk. Immediately his father sent his limousine to pick the man up, while his mother prepared the best guest room. Allan watched wide-eyed, as the beautiful coverlets were turned down on the exquisite, old four-poster bed, revealing the monogrammed sheets.

"But, Mother," he protested, "he's drunk. He might even get sick."

"I know," his mother replied kindly, "but this man has slipped and fallen. When he comes to, he will be so ashamed. He will need all the loving encouragement we can give him."[5]

People make mistakes, have bad days, and often fail to meet up to our expectations. This hits hardest when they are the ones we love the most. On those occasions, we must respond with kindness and forgiveness, rather than being critical and judgmental.

We have a saying around our house that applies to dealing with difficult circumstances, especially cantankerous people: *Reach way down deep*. When that vertical relationship with God is in place, you can "reach way down deep" and tap into a source that only God can provide.

So, there you have them, 19 *Faith ESSENTIALS*. I'm sure the list is incomplete. You've probably thought of others you would add. It is my fervent prayer, however, that they've helped to get you started, reset, or reassured in your walk with Christ.

ENDNOTES

Chapter One
[1] Raymond McHenry, *The Best of In Other Words* (Houston: Raymond McHenry Publisher, 1996), 30.
[2] Max Lucado, *In the Eye of the Storm*, (Dallas: Word Publishing, 1991), 153.

Chapter Two
[1] Paul E. Little, *Know What You Believe* (Downers Grove, IL: IVP Books, 2003), 47.
[2] Ibid.
[3] Ibid, 48.
[4] Ibib.,41.
[5] Herschel H. Hobbs, *What Baptists Believe* (Nashville, TN: Broadman Press, 1964), 17.
[6] M.R. DeHaan and H.G. *Bosch, Our Daily Bread* (Grand Rapids, MI: Zondervan, 1959), July 10.

Chapter Three
[1] Herschel H. Hobbs, *What Baptists Believe* (Nashville, TN: Broadman Press, 1964),
[2] Raymond McHenry, *The Best of In Other Words* (Houston: Raymond McHenry Publisher, 1996), 228.
[3] Mary B.C. Slade (words), Asa B. Everett (music), *Footsteps of Jesus.*

Chapter Four
[1] Erwin W. Lutzer, *The Serpent of Paradise* (Chicago: Moody Press, 1996), 24.
[2] Ibid, 26.
[3] Ibid, 27.
[4] Ibid, 45.
[5] John Phillips, *Exploring Genesis* (Chicago: Moody Press, 1980), 63.
[6] Jeff Spurrier, "Your Own Piece of Paradise." *Men's Journal* January 2005, 60-67.

Chapter Five
[1] *www.raindrop.org/rain/writings*

Chapter Six
[1] Leslie B. Flynn, *19 gifts of the Spirit* (Wheaton, IL: Victor Books, 1974),26.
[2] Herschel H. Hobbs, *Fundamentals of our Faith,* (Nashville, TN: Broadman & Holman, 1960), 61.
[3] Ibid.
[4] *www.thirstytheologian.com*
[5] *www.thesancydiamond.com/History.htm*

Chapter Seven

[1] Raymond McHenry, *The Best of In Other Words* (Houston: Raymond McHenry Publisher, 1996), 194.
[2] Dick Eastman, *The Hour that Changes the World* (Grand Rapids, MI: Chosen Books, 2009), 29.
[3] Peter Lord, *The 2959 Plan*, (Titusville, FL: Agape Ministries, 1976), 16.
[4] Dick Eastman, *The Hour that Changes the World* (Grand Rapids, MI: Chosen Books, 2009), 31.
[5] www.sermonillustrations.com/a-z/c/confessions.htm
[6] Ibid.

Chapter Eight

[1] Herschel H. Hobbs, *Fundamentals of our Faith* (Nashville, TN: Broadman & Holman, 1960), 127.
[2] Ibid, 128.
[3] Ibid, 127.
[4] M.R. Dehaan and H.G. Bosch, *Our Daily Bread* (Grand Rapids, MI: Zondervan, 1959), November 6.

Chapter Nine

[1] Stan Guthrie, *All That Jesus Asks* (Grand Rapids, MI: Baker Books, 2010)
[2] www.sermonillustrations.com

Chapter Ten

[1] www.new-testament-christian.com/ordinancebaptismandcommunion.html
[2] Ibid.
[3] www.sermonillustrations.com

Chapter Eleven

[1] David Jeremiah, *Searching for Heaven on Earth* (Nashville, TN: Integrity Publishers, 2004), 124.
[2] M.R. DeHann and H.G. Bosch, *Our Daily Bread* (Grand Rapids, MI: Daybreak Books, 1959).

Chapter Twelve

[1] Landrum P. Leavell, *Angels, Angels, Angels* (Nashville, TN: Broadman Press, 1973), 11.
[2] Billy Graham, *Angels, Angels, Angels, Angels* (Waco, TX: Word Books, 1986), 27.
[3] Landrum P. Leavell, *Angels, Angels, Angels* (Nashville, TN: Broadman Press, 1973), 15.
[4] Billy Graham, *Angels, Angels, Angels, Angels* (Waco, TX: Word Books, 1986), 100-101.
[5] Ibid, 17.

[6] John Phillips, *Exploring Genesis* (Chicago: Moody Press, 1980), 63.

[7] *www.sermonillustrations.com/a-z/a/angels.htm*

[8] Billy Graham, *Angels, Angels, Angels, Angels* (Waco, TX: Word Books, 1986), 33.

[9] Ibid, 34.

Chapter Thirteen

[1] *The Billy Graham Christian Worker's Handbook* (Minneapolis: World Wide Publications, 1984), 125.

[2] Ibid.

[3] Ibid.

[4] *www.history.navy*

[5] Charles R. Swindoll, *The Tale of the Tardy Oxcart* (Nashville: Word Publishing, 1998), 275.

Chapter Fourteen

[1] Ralph Hickok, Sports Biographies, "Martin, Pepper (John L.R.)," www.hickoksports.com/biograph/martinpepper.shtml.

[2] George Sweeting, *Psalms of the Heart* (Wheaton, IL: Victor Books, 1989) 70-71.

[3] Leon Morris, *Tyndale New Testament Commentaries: Luke* (Grand Rapids, MI: Eerdmans Publishing Co., 1974), 329).

[4] Randy Alcorn, *Heaven* (Wheaton, IL: Tyndale House Publishers, Inc., 2004) 42.

[5] Billy Graham, *Facing Death and the Life After* (Minneapolis, MN: Grason, 1987) 240.

[6] *www.sermonillustrations.com*

Chapter Fifteen

[1] George Ladd, *A Commentary on the Revelation* (Grand Rapids: 1972), 262.

[2] *www.associate,com*

Chapter Sixteen

[1] Robert Jeffress, *As Time Runs Out* (Nashville: Broadman & Holman, 1999), 127.

[2] Ibid. 149.

[3] Ibid. 160.

[4] Raymond McHenry, *The Best of In Other Words* (Houston: Raymond McHenry Publisher, 1996), 135.

Chapter Seventeen

[1] Randy Alcorn, *Heaven* (Wheaton, IL: Tyndale House Publishers, 2004), 31,32.

[2] Michael Green, *Tyndale New Testament Commentaries: 2 Peter and Jude* (Leicester, England; Grand Rapids: IVP, Eerdmans, 1983), 138.

Chapter Eighteen

[1] Randy Alcorn, *Heaven* (Wheaton, IL: Tyndale House Publishers, 2004), 242.

[2] *www.news.yahoo.com*

[3] Robert H. Mounce, *The Book of Revelation* (Grand Rapids: Eerdmans Publishing, 1977), 387.

[4] George Eldon Ladd, *A Commentary of the Revelation of John* (Grand Rapids: Eerdmans Publishing, 1972), 288.

5 Alcorn, 337.

[6] Ibid, 254.

[7] Ibid, 307.

[8] *www.beafutureleader.blogspot.com*

Chapter Nineteen

[1] Leon Morris, *Luke: Tyndale New Testament Commentaries* (Grand Rapids: Eerdman's Publishing, 1974), 188.

[2] M.R. DeHaan and H.G. Bosch, *Our Daily Bread* (Grand Rapids: Zondervan, 1959).

[3] Raymond McHenry, *The Best of In Other Word* (Houston: Raymond McHenry Publisher, 1996), 228.

[4] *Our Daily Bread* (Grand Rapids: Radio Bible Class, March 6, 1994).

[5] Billy Graham, *The Holy Spirit* (Minneapolis, MN: Grason, 1978), 190-191.